MELISSA LEAPMAN'S

DESIGNER CROCHET ACCESSORIES

Quarto is the authority on a wide range of topics.

Quarto educates, entertains and enriches the lives of our readers—enthusiasts and lovers of hands-on liv

www.QuartoKnows.com

First published in the United States of America in 2016 by
Creative Publishing international, an imprint of
Quarto Publishing Group USA Inc.
400 First Avenue North
Suite 400
Minneapolis, MN 55401
1-800-328-3895
QuartoKnows.com
Visit our blogs at QuartoKnows.com

10 9 8 7 6 5 4 3 2 1

ISBN: 978-1-58923-928-9

Digital edition published in 2016
eISBN: 978-1-63159-152-5

Library of Congress Cataloging-in-Publication Data available

Design: Stacy Wakefield Forte

Printed in China

+

DEDICATION

To Patty Olson—You never
fail to make me smile.

+

ACKNOWLEDGMENTS

I am grateful to the following expert crocheters who stitched the project samples to be photographed: Fran Elsky, Danelle Howard, Susan Jeffers, Cheryl Keeley, and Joyce Pearson. I would not have had a book without you!

Extra kudos go to the Amazing Danelle Howard for her special contribution to the book. You rock, Girl!

Many thanks, too, go to the yarn and button companies that supplied the beautiful materials used to create these accessories. For the past thirty (!) years, you have supported and inspired me. Thank you!

MELISSA LEAPMAN'S

DESIGNER CROCHET ACCESSORIES

fresh, new designs for

HATS + SCARVES + COWLS
SHAWLS + HANDBAGS + JEWELRY

and more

Creative Publishing international

CONTENTS

INTRODUCTION

Fashionistas have finally confirmed what avid crocheters have known all along: Our beloved needleart is not only a time-honored craft, it's also a vibrant fiber art that's beautiful, practical, and very, very "now." **+** This designer collection showcases twenty-five up-to-the-minute, fun-to-stitch, and easy-to-wear fashion accessories for women, from an ultra-chunky cropped capelet to a funky beaded wrap bracelet, to a retro-glam semicircular shawl, and more. Each project combines basic crochet techniques with today's most exciting yarns to spruce up your wardrobe—and fill your project bag!—year round. **+** When my paternal grandmother, Ada Leapman, taught me this craft when I was four, I bet she never imagined we'd see New York and European couture and designer houses featuring crocheted fashion on the catwalk, but apparently, some folks knew it all along. **+** This book is for us. **+ LET'S CROCHET!**

PROJECTS

THIS SECTION CONTAINS TWENTY-FIVE ON-TREND DESIGNER PROJECTS, FROM A MODERN FAIR ISLE–STYLE WINTER HAT TO A USEFUL TOTE BAG TO A LIGHT-AS-AIR (BUT TOASTY WARM) INFINITY COWL.

WHICH WILL YOU STITCH FIRST?

HADLEY

ARAN-INSPIRED CABLED SHOULDER BAG

Showcase your cabling prowess while making this useful shoulder bag. Every other row consists of simple and mindless half double crochet stitches. No one will ever know that you had to concentrate for only half the rows!

+

SIZE

One size

+

FINISHED MEASUREMENTS

Approximately 10" (25.5 cm) wide × 9½" (24 cm) deep

+

MATERIALS

• Plymouth Yarn *Homestead Tweed* [100% wool: 3½ oz/ 100 g (194 yd/ 177.5 m), 3 hanks of #526 Thistle]

• Crochet hook sizes H/8 (5 mm) and I/9 (5.5 mm), or size needed to obtain gauge

• Blunt-end yarn needle

• Coordinating fabric for lining, ½ yd (.46 m), optional

+

GAUGE

With the larger hook, 14 sts and 12 rows in pattern = 4" (10 cm). To save time, take time to check gauge.

+

ALTERNATIVE YARN CHOICE

Lion Brand *Heartland Tweed*

NOTES

- Always skip the hdc behind the FPsts.
- Each FPtr, FPdc, and FPdtr counts as FPsts.
- Popcorn = Work 5 double crochet stitches in a stitch or space, drop the loop from the hook, reinsert the hook in the first double crochet stitch made, pick up the dropped loop and pull it through the first double crochet stitch (page 131).

BACK

Chain 36.

Foundation Row 1 (RS): Hdc in the third ch from the hook and in each ch across, turn—35 hdc.

Foundation Row 2: Ch 2 (counts as hdc here and throughout), skip the first st, hdc in each st across, ending with hdc in top of turning-ch-2, turn.

Row 1 (RS): Ch 2, skip the first hdc, hdc in each of the next 2 hdc, FPtr in the next st 2 rows below, skip the hdc after the last hdc made, hdc in each of the next 3 hdc, FPtr in the next st 2 rows below, skip the hdc after the last hdc made, hdc in each of the next 2 hdc, FPtr in each of the next 2 sts 2 rows below, skip 2 hdc after the last hdc made, hdc in each of the next 3 hdc, FPtr in each of the next 2 sts 2 rows below, skip 2 hdc after the last hdc made, hdc in the next hdc, FPtr in each of the next 2 sts 2 rows below, skip 2 hdc after the last hdc made, hdc in each of the next 3 hdc, FPtr in each of the next 2 sts 2 rows below, skip 2 hdc after the last hdc made, hdc in each of the next 2 hdc, FPtr in the next st 2 rows below, skip the hdc after the last hdc made, hdc in each of the next 3 hdc, FPtr in the next st 2 rows below, skip the hdc after the last hdc made, hdc in each of the next 2 hdc, hdc in the top of the turning-ch-2, turn.

Row 2 and all WS rows: Ch 2, skip the first hdc, hdc in each st across, ending with hdc in top of turning-ch-2, turn.

Row 3: Ch 2, skip the first hdc, hdc in each of the next 2 hdc, FPtr in the next st 2 rows below, skip the hdc after the last hdc made, hdc in the next hdc, Popcorn in the next hdc, hdc in the next hdc, FPtr in the next st 2 rows below, skip the hdc after the last hdc made, hdc in each of the next 4 hdc, FPdtr in the 2 skipped FPsts 2 rows below, skip 2 hdc after the last hdc made, hdc in the next hdc, skip the next 3 hdc, FPdtr in the next 2 FPsts 2 rows below, skip 2 hdc after the last hdc made, hdc in the next hdc, *working behind the last 2 FPsts made* (page 135), FPdtr in each of the 2 skipped FPsts 2 rows below, skip 2 hdc after the last hdc made, hdc in the next hdc, skip the next 2 hdc, FPdtr in each of the next 2 FPsts 2 rows below, skip 2 hdc after the last hdc

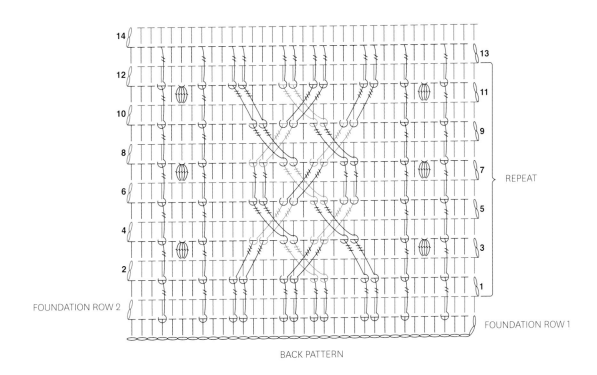

14

13

12

11

10

9

8

7 REPEAT

6

5

4

3

2

1

FOUNDATION ROW 2

FOUNDATION ROW 1

BACK PATTERN

made, hdc in each of the next 4 hdc, FPtr in the next st 2 rows below, skip the hdc after the last hdc made, hdc in the next hdc, Popcorn in the next hdc, hdc in the next hdc, FPtr in the next st 2 rows below, skip the hdc after the last hdc made, hdc in each of the next 2 hdc, hdc in the top of the turning-ch-2. Ch 2, turn.

Row 5: Ch 2, skip the first hdc, hdc in each of the next 2 hdc, FPtr in the next st 2 rows below, skip the

hdc after the last hdc made, hdc in each of the next 3 hdc, FPtr in the next st 2 rows below, skip the hdc after the last hdc made, hdc in each of the next 4 hdc, [skip the next 3 hdc, FPdtr in each of the next 2 FPsts 2 rows below, skip 2 hdc after the last hdc made, hdc in the next hdc, *working in front of the last 2 FPsts made* (page 135), FPdtr in each of the 2 skipped FPsts 2 rows below, skip 2 hdc after the last hdc made, hdc in the next hdc] twice, hdc in each of the next 3 hdc, FPtr in the next st 2 rows below, skip the hdc after the last hdc made, hdc in each of the next 3 hdc, FPtr in the next st 2 rows below, skip the hdc after the last hdc made, hdc in each of the next 2 hdc, hdc in the top of the turning-ch-2. Ch 2, turn.

Row 7: Ch 2, skip the first hdc, hdc in each of the next 2 hdc, FPtr in the next st 2 rows below, skip the hdc after the last hdc made, hdc in the next hdc, Popcorn in the next hdc, hdc in the next hdc, FPtr in the next st 2 rows below, skip the hdc after the last hdc made, hdc in each of the next 4 hdc, FPtr in each of the next 2 FPsts 2 rows below, skip 2 hdc after the last hdc made, hdc in the next hdc, skip the next 3 hdc, FPdtr in the next 2 FPsts 2 rows below, skip 2 hdc after the last hdc made, hdc in the next hdc, working behind the last 2 FPsts made, FPdtr in each of the 2 skipped FPsts 2 rows below, skip 2 hdc after the last hdc made, hdc in the next hdc, FPtr in each of the next 2 FPsts 2 rows below, skip 2 hdc after the last hdc made, hdc in each of the next 4 hdc, FPtr in the next st 2 rows below, skip the hdc after the last hdc made, hdc in the next hdc, Popcorn in the next hdc, hdc in the next hdc, FPtr in the next st 2 rows below, skip the hdc after the last hdc made, hdc in each of the next 2 hdc, hdc in the top of the turning-ch-2. Ch 2, turn.

Row 9: Same as Row 5. Ch 2, turn.

Row 11: Ch 2, skip the first hdc, hdc in each of the next 2 hdc, FPtr in the next st 2 rows below, skip the hdc after the last hdc made, hdc in the next hdc, Popcorn in the next hdc, hdc in the next hdc, FPtr in the next st 2 rows below, skip the hdc after the last hdc made, hdc in each of the next 2 hdc, skip the next 3 hdc, FPdtr in each of the next 2 FPsts 2 rows below, skip 2 hdc after the last hdc made, hdc in each of the next 3 hdc, skip the next 3 hdc, FPdtr in the next 2 FPsts 2 rows below, skip 2 hdc after the last hdc made, hdc in the next hdc, *working behind the last 2 FPsts made*, FPdtr in each of the 2 skipped FPsts 2 rows below, skip 2 hdc after the last hdc made, hdc in each of the next 3 hdc, FPdtr in each of the 2 skipped FPsts 2 rows below, skip 2 hdc after the last hdc made, hdc in each of the next 2 hdc, FPtr in the next st 2 rows below, skip the hdc after the last hdc made, hdc in the next hdc, Popcorn in the next hdc, hdc in the next hdc, FPtr in the next st 2 rows below, skip the hdc after the last hdc made, hdc in each of the next 2 hdc, hdc in the top of the turning-ch-2. Ch 2, turn.

Row 12: Same as Row 2.

Rows 13–56: Work Rows 1–12 three times, then work Rows 1–8.

Fasten off.

FRONT

Work same as the back until the front measures approximately 8" (20.5 cm) from the beginning, ending with Row 12 of the pattern.

Fasten off.

FINISHING

STRAP/GUSSET

With the smaller hook, ch 7.

Foundation Row: Sc in the second ch from the hook and in each ch across—6 sc, turn.

Row 1: Ch 1, sc in each sc across, turn.

Repeat Row 1 until the strap/gusset measures approximately 60" (152.5 cm) from the beginning. Fasten off.

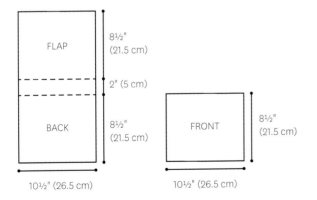

Block pieces to measurements.

With the right side facing, sew the Foundation Row to the last row of the strap/gusset.

With the right side facing and centering the strap/gusset seam at the center bottom of front, sew one side of the strap/gusset to front.

Sew the other side of strap/gusset to back, leaving 10½" (26.5 cm) unsewn on each side for the top flap.

Optional: Cut lining to fit the bag, including the flap, plus ¼" (6 mm) seam allowance on all sides. Cut lining to fit the inside of the strap, plus ¼" (6 mm) seam allowance on all sides. Sew the lining in place, folding ¼" (6 mm) hems to the wrong side.

EDGING

Row 1: With the right side facing and the smaller hook, attach the yarn with a slip st to the edge of top flap and ch 1, work 35 sc evenly spaced along the edge of the flap, *do not turn.*

Row 2: Ch 1, working from left to right, reverse sc (page 131) in each st across the edge of the flap. Fasten off.

Work edging across the top edge of front same as for the flap.

MINERVA

SEMICIRCULAR SHAWL

Crocheted from the top down, this spectacular shawl is surprisingly easy to stitch. Its stitch pattern is easily memorized after just a few rows!

+
SIZE
One size

+
FINISHED MEASUREMENTS
54" (137 cm) wide and 27" (68.5 cm) deep, blocked

+
MATERIALS
• Koigu *KPM Handpainted* Solids
[100% merino wool; each approximately 1.75 oz/50 g and 175 yds/160 m) 7 skeins in #2340S]

• Crochet hook size F/5 (3.75 mm) or size needed to obtain gauge

+
GAUGE
18 dc in pattern = 4" (10 cm).
To save time, take time to check gauge.

+
ALTERNATIVE YARN CHOICE
Louet *Gems* Fingering Weight

NOTE

- In order to ensure random color distribution, alternate between two different balls of yarn, working two rows from each. Carry the yarns loosely up the side of the shawl.

SPECIAL STITCHES

Reverse Single Crochet (reverse sc) = *Working from left to right*, insert hook in next stitch, yarn over, draw up a loop; yarn over hook and draw loop through both loops on hook (page 135).

CONTINUE IN PATTERN THROUGH ROW 63, ADDING ONE DC TO EACH SPOKE IN EACH RND

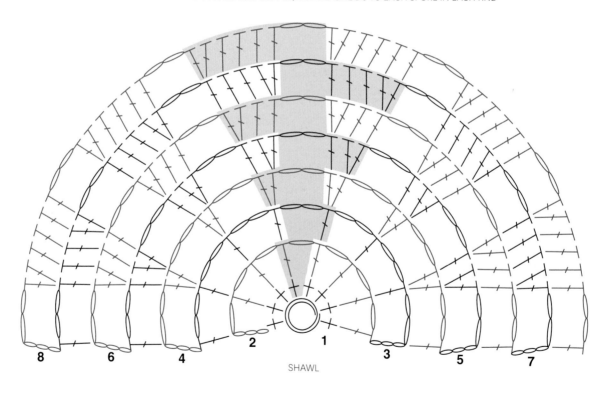

SHAWL

SHAWL

Begin with an adjustable ring (page 129).

Row 1 (RS): Ch 1, work 8 sc in the adjustable ring, turn.

Row 2: Ch 4 (counts as dc, ch 1), skip the first sc, *dc in the next sc, ch 1; repeat from the * across, ending with dc in the last sc, turn—7 ch-1 sps.

Row 3: Ch 5 (counts as dc, ch 2 here and throughout), skip the first dc, *dc in the next dc, ch 2, skip next ch-1 sp; repeat from the * across, ending with dc in the third ch of the turning-ch-4, turn.

Row 4: Ch 5, skip the first dc, *2 dc in the next dc, ch 2, skip next ch-2 sp; repeat from the * across, ending with dc in the third ch of the turning-ch-5, turn.

Row 5: Ch 5, skip the first dc, *2 dc in the next dc, dc in the next dc, ch 2, skip next ch-2 sp; repeat from the * across, ending with dc in the third ch of the turning-ch-5, turn.

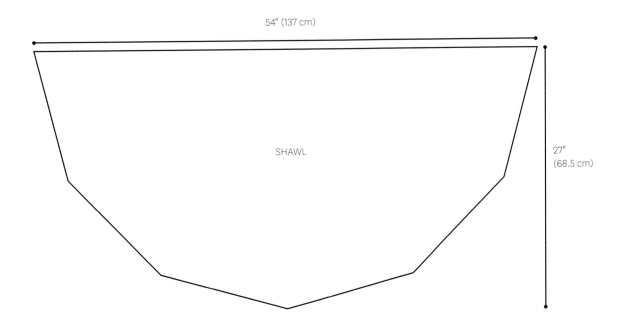

54" (137 cm)

SHAWL

27" (68.5 cm)

Row 6: Ch 5, skip the first dc, *2 dc in the next dc, dc in each of the next 2 dc, ch 2, skip next ch-2 sp; repeat from the * across, ending with dc in the third ch of the turning-ch-5, turn—4 dc in each section.

Row 7: Ch 5, skip the first dc, *2 dc in the next dc, dc in each dc across to next ch-2 sp, ch 2, skip next ch-2 sp; repeat from the * across, ending with dc in the third ch of the turning-ch-5, turn—5 dc in each section.

Rows 8–63: Rep Row 7—61 dc in each section at end of last row.

EDGING

Row 64: Ch 1, sc in the first dc, ch 4, skip the next ch-2 sp, *[sc in the next dc, ch 4, skip the next 2 dc] 20 times, sc in the next dc, ch 4, skip the next ch-2 sp; repeat from the * across, ending with sc in the third ch of the turning-ch-5, turn—127 ch-4 sps.

Row 65: Ch 1, slip st in the first sc, *5 sc in the next ch-4 sp; repeat from the * across, ending with slip st in the last sc.

Fasten off.

UPPER EDGING

Row 1: With the RS facing, attach the yarn with a slip st to the upper right-hand edge, and ch 1, work 222 sc evenly spaced across the upper edge of the shawl, taking care that the fabric doesn't pucker or ripple, do not turn.

Row 2: Ch 1, working from left to right, reverse sc (page 135) in each st across. Fasten off.

FINISHING

Weave in ends. Block to finished measurements.

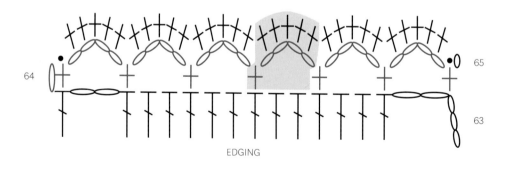

EDGING

COLLAFIRTH

FAIR ISLE-STYLE SKI HAT

The colorwork in this little cap mimics traditional Fair Isle patterns. If you'd prefer a slouchier version, just work one more repeat of the chart before starting the decreases for the crown.

+

SIZE

One size

+

FINISHED MEASUREMENTS

7½" (19 cm) tall; 19" (48.5 cm) in circumference

+

MATERIALS

• Plymouth Yarn *Select Worsted Merino Superwash* 〔4〕 (100% superwash merino wool; each approximately 3.5 oz/100 g and 218 yd/ 199.5 m), one hank each of #67 Medium Charcoal (A), #1 Natural (B), #7 Light Gray (C), and #18 Lavender (D)

• Crochet hook H/8 (5 mm) or size needed to obtain gauge

+

GAUGE

20 sts and 20 rows in band pattern = 4" (10 cm); 18 sts and 16 rows in crown pattern = 4" (10 cm). To save time, take time to check gauge.

+

ALTERNATIVE YARN CHOICE

Caron *Simply Soft Yarn*

NOTES

- Each round of crown is worked with the right side facing.

- All single crochet stitches except for those in the set-up round are worked in the back loop only.

- When changing colors, finish the last stitch of the old color with the new color when there are two loops on the hook.

- When working with one color, the other color is loosely carried along the wrong side of the fabric until it is needed again.

- On each round of crown, work over the yarn floats of the previous round, enclosing them inside the fabric.

CHART KEY

■ = SC IN MEDIUM GRAY (A)

☐ = SC IN NATURAL (B)

▨ = SC IN LIGHT GRAY (C)

▨ = SC IN LAVENDER (D)

CHART

SPECIAL STITCHES

Single Crochet 2 Together (sc2tog) = [Insert the hook in next stitch and draw up a loop] twice, yarn over and draw through all 3 loops on hook (page 133).

STITCH PATTERN

Sideways Rib Pattern (over any number of stitches)

Foundation Row (RS): Sc in second ch from hook and in each ch across, turn.

Row 1: Ch 1, sc in *the back loop only* of each sc across, turn.

Repeat the Row 1 for pattern.

HAT

Leaving a 12" (30.5 cm) tail, with A, ch 8.

BAND

Begin Sideways Rib Pattern, and work even on 7 sts until the piece, when slightly stretched, measures approximately 19" (48.5 cm) from beg. *Do not fasten off.*

Turn the piece sideways and use the yarn tail to whipstitch (page 139) the first and last rows together, creating a ring.

Set Up Round (RS): Working along the side of ribbed

ring, and continuing with Color A, ch 1, and work 78 sc evenly spaced across side edge of band. Place a marker for the beginning of the round.

Round 1 (RS): Ch 1, *working in the back loop only,* work Round 1 of the Fair Isle Pattern, working from A to B, then repeat working from A to B around, join with a slip st in top of first sc.

Rounds 2–9: Ch 1, *working in the back loop only,* work Rounds 2–9 of the Fair Isle pattern. At the end of each round, join with a slip st to the first st.

Rounds 10–14: Work Rounds 1–5 of the Fair Isle pattern. At the end of each round, join with a slip st to the first st.

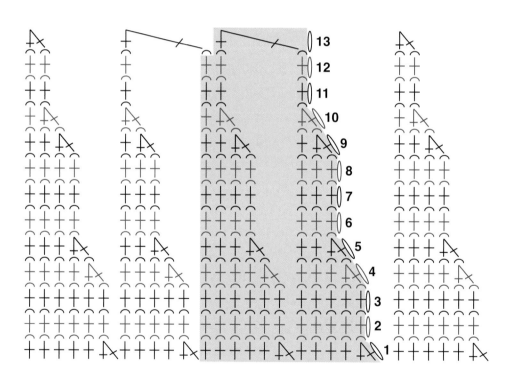

CROWN
DECREASE PATTERN

CROWN

Round 1 (Decrease Round): Working with A only, ch 1, *sc2tog over next 2 sts, sc in each of the next 4 sts, sc2tog over next 2 sts, sc in each of the next 5 sts; repeat from * around; join with a slip st in the first sc—66 sts.

Rounds 2 and 3: Ch 1, work Rounds 7 and 8 of the Fair Isle Pattern; join with a slip st in the first sc.

Round 4 (Decrease Round): Working with A only, ch 1, *sc2tog over next 2 sts, sc in each of the next 3 sts, sc2tog over next 2 sts, sc in each of the next 4 sts; repeat from * around, change to B, join with a slip st in the first sc—54 sts.

Round 5 (Decrease Round): Working with B only, ch 1, *sc2tog over next 2 sts, sc in each of the next 2 sts, sc2tog over next 3 sts; repeat from * around; join with a slip st in the first sc—42 sts.

Rounds 6–8: Ch 1, work Rounds 2–4 of the Fair Isle Pattern; join with a slip st in the first sc.

Round 9 (Decrease Round): Working with Color B only, ch 1, *sc2tog over next 2 sts, sc in the next st, sc2tog over next 2 sts, sc in each of the next 2 sts; repeat from * around, change to A, join with a slip st in the first sc—30 sts.

Round 10 (Decrease Round): Working with Color A only, ch 1, *[sc2tog over next 2 sts] twice, sc in the next st; repeat from * around; join with a slip st in the first sc—18 sts.

Rounds 11 and 12: Ch 1, work Rounds 7 and 8 of the Fair Isle Pattern; join with a slip st in the first sc.

Round 13 (Decrease Round): Working with A only, ch 1, *sc2tog over next 2 sts; repeat from * around; join with a slip st in the first sc—9 sts.

Fasten off, leaving an 8" (20.5 cm) tail. With yarn needle, weave tail through the tops of the remaining 9 sts and pull tight to secure.

FINISHING

Weave in ends.

BENEDETTA

TOP-DOWN TRIANGULAR SHAWL

Wrap yourself (or a loved one!) in this lacy shawl. It's worked from the top down, with each row getting successively shorter.

+
SIZE
One size

+
FINISHED MEASUREMENTS
54" (137 cm) wide and 25" (63.5 cm) deep, blocked.

+
MATERIALS
• Classic Elite *Fresco* (60% wool/30% baby alpaca/10% angora; each approximately 1.75 oz/50 g and 164 yards/151 m), 5 hanks in #5349 Blue Teal

• Crochet hook size G/6 (4 mm) or size needed to obtain gauge

+
GAUGE
Each 7-dc group = 1" (2.5 cm); 2 repeats in pattern = 2" (5 cm) wide; 6 rows in pattern = 4½" (11.5 cm). To save time, take time to check gauge.

+
ALTERNATIVE YARN CHOICE
Malabrigo *Sock*

SHAWL

Ch 252.

Foundation Row (RS): Sc in the second ch from the hook and in the next ch, *ch 3, skip the next 3 ch, [dc, ch 3, dc] in the next ch, ch 3, skip the next 3 ch, sc in each of the next 3 ch; repeat from the * across, ending with ch 3, skip the next 3 ch, [dc, ch 3, dc] in the next ch, ch 3, skip the next 3 ch, sc in each of the last 2 ch, turn—25 repeats.

Foundation Row 2 (WS): Ch 3, skip the first ch-3 sp, *7 dc in the next ch-3 sp, ch 3, skip the next sc, sc in the next sc, ch 3, skip the next ch-3 sp; repeat from the * across, ending with 7 dc in the next ch-3 sp, ch 3, skip the next ch-3 sp, skip the next sc, slip st in the last sc, turn.

Row 1: Slip st in each of the first 3 ch, slip st in each of the next 3 dc, sc in each of the next 4 sc, *ch 5, sc in each of the next 7 dc; repeat from the * across, ending with ch 5, sc in each of the next 4 dc, turn, leaving remaining sts unworked.

Row 2: Slip st in the first sc, ch 3, *[dc, ch 3, dc] in the next ch-5 sp, ch 3, skip the next 2 sc, sc in

FOUNDATION ROW 2

FOUNDATION ROW 1

REPEAT

each of the next 3 sc, ch 3; repeat from the * across, ending with [dc, ch 3, dc] in the next ch-5 sp, ch 3, skip the next 3 sc, slip st in the last sc, turn.

Row 3: Ch 3, skip the first ch-3 sp, *7 dc in the next ch-3 sp, ch 3, skip the next sc, sc in the next sc, ch 3, skip the next ch-3 sp; repeat from the * across, ending with 7 dc in the next ch-3 sp, ch 3, skip the next ch-3 sp, slip st in the last sc, turn.

Rows 4–69: Repeat Rows 1–3 twenty-three times.

Row 70: Slip st in each of the first 3 ch, slip st in each of the next 3 dc, sc in each of the next 4 sc, ch 5, sc in each of the next 4 dc, turn, leaving remaining sts unworked.

Row 71: Slip st in the first sc, ch 3, [dc, ch 3, dc] in the next ch-5 sp, ch 3, skip the next 3 sc, slip st in the last sc, turn.

Row 72: Ch 3, skip first ch-3 sp, 7 dc in the next ch-3 sp, ch 3, skip the next ch-3 sp, slip st in the last sc, turn. Fasten off.

EDGING

LOWER EDGING

Row 1 (WS): With the WS facing, attach yarn with a slip st to the beginning of Row 1, ch 1, sc in the same st as the slip st, *ch 7, skip the next ch-3 sp, skip the next 3 dc, sc in the next sc; repeat from the * across side edge to the lower point, ch 7, skip the next ch-3 sp, skip the next 3 dc, sc in the next dc, **ch 7, skip the next 3 dc, sc in the next sc; repeat from the ** across the other side edge, turn.

Work now progresses in the round.

Round 2 (RS): Ch 1, sc in the first sc, [2 sc, 2 hdc, 2 dc, tr, 2 dc, 2 hdc, 2 sc] in Row 1 of Edging, working across the straight top edge of the shawl, work 3 sc in the corner, *working across opposite side of the Foundation Chain, sc in the next ch, 3 sc in the next ch-3 sp, sc in the next ch**, 3 sc in the next ch-3 sp, sc in each of the next 3 ch; repeat from the * across, ending the last repeat at **, sc in each of the last 2 ch, 3 sc in the corner st; join with a slip st in the first sc. Fasten off.

FINISHING

Weave in ends. Block to the finished measurements.

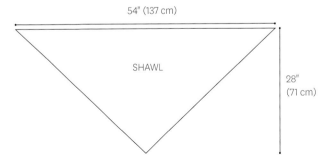

54" (137 cm)

SHAWL

28" (71 cm)

COSI

KEYHOLE SCARF

Made out of an amazingly lightweight wool-blend yarn,

this keyhole scarf features an easily memorized stitch pattern

that is reversible and will trap in warmth.

+
SIZE
One size

+
FINISHED MEASUREMENTS
6¼" (16 cm) wide ×
35" (89 cm) long, blocked

+
MATERIALS
• Classic Elite
Avalanche
🔲
(42% alpaca/
42% wool/16% nylon;
each approximately
1.75 oz/50 g and
200 yd/183 m),
2 balls of #1254 Sky

• Crochet hook size
K/10.5 (6.5 mm) or
size needed to
obtain gauge

+
GAUGE
15 sts and 12 rows
in pattern = 4" (10 cm),
blocked. To save time,
take time to check gauge.

+
ALTERNATIVE YARN CHOICE
Lion Brand
Fishermen's Wool

SCARF

Chain 25.

Foundation Row (RS): Dc in the fourth ch from the hook and in each ch across, turn—23 sts.

Row 1: Ch 2 (counts as hdc here and throughout), skip the first st, *FPdc in the next st, BPdc in the next st; repeat from the * 9 times, FPdc in the next st, hdc in the top of the turning-ch-2, turn—23 sts.

Repeat the Row 1 until the piece measures approximately 27" (68.5 cm) from the beginning.

MAKE KEYHOLE

Next Row: Ch 2 (counts as hdc here and throughout), skip the first st, *FPdc in the next st, BPdc in the next st*; repeat from the * to * twice, FPdc in the next st, ch 7, skip the next 7 sts, rep from * to * 3 times, FPdc in the next st, hdc in the top of the turning-ch-2, turn—23 sts.

Next Row: Ch 2 (counts as hdc here and throughout), skip the first st, *FPdc in the next st, BPdc in the next st*; repeat from the * to * twice, FPdc in the next st, 7 hdc in next ch-7 sp, rep from * to * 3 times, FPdc in the next st, hdc in the top of the turning-ch-2, turn—23 sts.

Repeat Row 1 until the piece measures approximately 35" (89 cm) from the beginning. Fasten off.

FINISHING

Weave in ends. Block to the finished measurements.

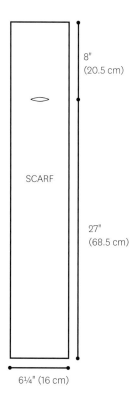

8"
(20.5 cm)

SCARF

27"
(68.5 cm)

6¼" (16 cm)

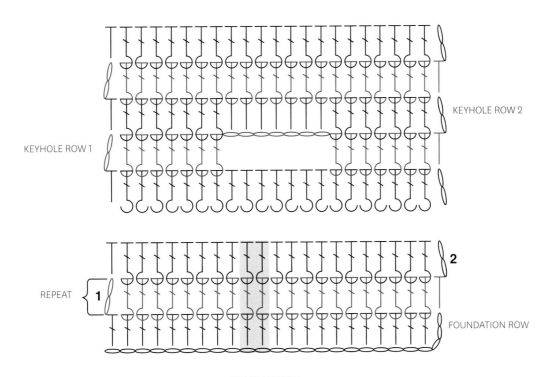

KEYHOLE ROW 2

KEYHOLE ROW 1

REPEAT

1

2

FOUNDATION ROW

SCARF PATTERN

FOGLIE

SKINNY SUMMER FASHION SCARF

You'll grab this little openwork scarf year round. Named for the Italian word for "leaves," it is constructed out of two identical pieces that are made from the bottom up and then sewn together at the center back.

+
SIZE
One size

+
**FINISHED
MEASUREMENTS**
6½" (16.5 cm) wide ×
53" (134.5 cm) long,
blocked

+
MATERIALS
• Cascade
Ultra Pima Fine

(100% pima cotton;
each approximately
1.75 oz/50 g and
136 yd/124.5 m),
3 balls of #3758
Soft Sage

• Crochet hook size
E/4 (3.5 mm) or
size needed to
obtain gauge

• Blunt-end yarn needle

+
GAUGE
5 dc = 1" (2.5 cm);
6 rows in pattern =
4" (10 cm).
To save time, take time
to check gauge.

+
**ALTERNATIVE
YARN CHOICE**
Patons *Grace*

FIRST HALF

Chain 41.

Foundation Row (RS): Dc in the fourth ch from the hook, ch 1, skip the next ch, dc in the next ch, ch 2, skip the next ch, 2 dc in the next ch, ch 2, skip the next 2 ch, dc in each of the next 6 ch, ch 2, skip the next 2 ch, dc2tog over the next 2 ch, ch 1, skip the next 3 ch, dc2tog over the next 2 ch, ch 2, skip the next 2 ch, dc in each of the next 6 ch, ch 2, skip the next 2 ch, 2 dc in the next ch, ch 2, skip the next ch, dc in the next ch, ch 1, skip the next ch, dc in each of the last 2 ch. Ch 3, turn.

Row 1 (WS): Skip the first dc, dc in the next dc, ch 2, skip the next ch-1 sp, dc in the next dc, ch 2, skip the next ch-2 sp, 2 dc in each of the next 2 dc, ch 2, skip the next ch-2 sp, dc2tog over the next 2 dc, dc in each of the next 2 dc, dc2tog over the next 2 dc, ch 2, skip the next ch-2 sp, dc2tog over the next 2 sts, ch 2, skip the next ch-2 sp, dc2tog over the next 2 dc, dc in each of the next 2 dc, dc2tog over the next 2 dc, ch 2, skip the next ch-2 sp, 2 dc in each of the next 2 dc, ch 2, skip the next ch-2 sp, dc in the next dc, ch 2, skip the next ch-1 sp, dc in the next dc, dc in the top of the turning-ch-3. Ch 3, turn.

Row 2: Skip the first dc, dc in the next dc, ch 2, skip the next ch-2 sp, dc in the next dc, ch 2, skip the next ch-2 sp, 2 dc in the next dc, dc in each of the next 2 dc, 2 dc in the next dc, ch 2, skip the next ch-2 sp, [dc2tog over the next 2 sts] twice, ch 3, skip the next ch-2 sp, skip the next dc2tog, skip the next ch-2 sp, [dc2tog over the next 2 sts] twice, ch 2, skip the next ch-2 sp, 2 dc in the next dc, dc in each of the next 2 dc, 2 dc in the next dc, ch 2, skip the next ch-2 sp, dc in the next dc, ch 2, skip the next ch-2 sp, dc in the next dc, dc in the top of the turning-ch-3. Ch 3, turn.

Row 3: Skip the first dc, dc in the next dc, ch 1, skip the next ch, dc in the next ch, ch 2, 2 dc in the next dc, ch 2, skip the next ch-2 sp, dc in each of the next 6 dc, ch 2, skip the next ch-2 sp, dc2tog to combine the next 2 dc2tog, ch 1, skip the next ch-3 sp, dc2tog to combine the next 2 dc2tog, ch 2, skip the next ch-2 sp, dc in each of the next 6 dc, ch 2, skip the next ch-2 sp, 2 dc in the next dc, ch 2, dc in the next ch, ch 1, skip the next ch, dc in the next dc, dc in the top of the turning-ch-3. Ch 3, turn.

Row 4: Skip the first dc, dc in the next dc, ch 2, skip the next ch-1 sp, dc in the next dc, ch 2, skip the next ch-2 sp, 2 dc in each of the next 2 dc, ch 2, skip the next ch-2 sp, dc2tog over the next 2 dc, dc in each of the next 2 dc, dc2tog over the next 2 dc, ch 2, skip the next ch-2 sp, dc2tog over the next 2 dc2tog, ch 2, skip the next ch-2 sp, dc2tog over the next 2 dc, dc in each of the next 2 dc, dc2tog over

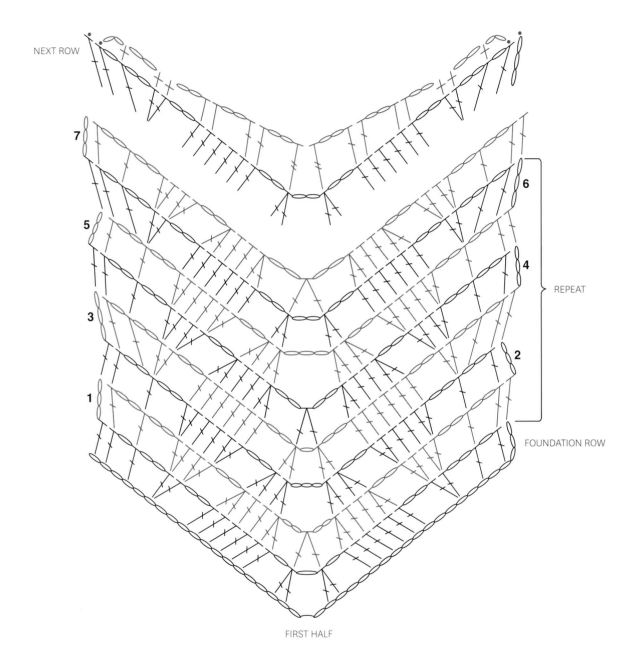

NEXT ROW

7

5

3

1

6

4

2

REPEAT

FOUNDATION ROW

FIRST HALF

the next 2 dc, ch 2, skip the next ch-2 sp, 2 dc in each of the next 2 dc, ch 2, skip the next ch-2 sp, dc in the next dc, skip the next ch-1 sp, ch 2, dc in the next dc, dc in the top of the turning-ch-3. Ch 3, turn.

Row 5: Skip the first dc, dc in the next dc, ch 2, skip the next ch-2 sp, dc in the next dc, ch 2, skip the next ch-2 sp, 2 dc in the next dc, dc in each of the next 2 dc, 2 dc in the next dc, ch 2, skip the next ch-2 sp, [dc2tog over the next 2 sts] twice, ch 3, skip the next ch-2 sp, skip the next dc2tog, skip the next ch-2 sp, [dc2tog over the next 2 sts] twice, ch 2, skip the next ch-2 sp, 2 dc in the next dc, dc in each of the next 2 dc, 2 dc in the next dc, ch 2, skip the next ch-2 sp, dc in the next dc, ch 2, skip the next ch-2 sp, dc in the next dc, dc in the top of the turning-ch-3. Ch 3, turn.

Row 6: Skip the first dc, dc in the next dc, ch 1, skip the next ch, dc in the next ch, ch 2, 2 dc in the next dc, ch 2, skip the next ch-2 sp, dc in each of the next 6 dc, ch 2, skip the next ch-2 sp, dc2tog over the next 2 dc2tog, ch 2, skip the next ch-3 sp, dc2tog over the next 2 dc2tog, ch 2, skip the next ch-2 sp, dc in each of the next 6 dc, ch 2, skip the next ch-2 sp, 2 dc in the next dc, ch 2, dc in the next ch, ch 1, skip the next ch, dc in the next dc, dc in the top of the turning-ch-3. Ch 3, turn.

Repeat Rows 1–6 for the pattern until the piece measures approximately 24" (61 cm), ending after Row 6 of the pattern. *Do not chain.* Turn.

Next Row (WS): Slip st in each of the first 2 dc, ch 2, sc in the next dc, ch 2, sc in each of the next 2 dc, ch 2, hdc in each of the next 2 dc, ch 2, skip the next 2 dc, dc in each of the next 2 dc, ch 2, tr in the next dc2tog, skip the next ch-2 sp, tr in the next dc2tog, ch 2, dc in each of the next 2 dc, ch 2, skip the next 2 dc, hdc in each of the next 2 dc, ch 2, sc in each of

6½"
(16.5 cm)

SCARF

53" (134.5 cm)

the next 2 dc, ch 2, sc in the next dc, ch 2, slip st in the next dc, slip st in the top of the turning-ch-3.

Fasten off.

SECOND HALF

Work same as the first half.

FINISHING

With the right sides together, matching sts, whip-stitch the last row of two halves together.

EDGING

With RS facing, join yarn with slip st in any corner, ch 1, *3 sc in corner st, sc evenly across to next corner; repeat from * around, join with slip st in first sc.

Weave in ends. Block to the finished measurements.

CELESTIA

AIRY INFINITY COWL

Although light as air, this ethereal cowl will keep you — or a lucky gift recipient — warm and cozy. The frilly chain-loop edging makes it especially feminine and adds an air of nostalgia.

+
SIZE

One size

+
FINISHED MEASUREMENTS

8" (20.5 cm) deep ×
56" (142 cm)
in circumference

+
MATERIALS

• Berroco *Briza*

(51% mohair/43% nylon/
6% wool; each
approximately
1.41 oz/40 g and
219 yd/200 m),
2 balls of #9315 Napa

• Crochet hook size
G/6 (4 mm) or
size needed
to obtain gauge

+
GAUGE

12 sts (1 repeat) =
2¼" (5.5 cm);
4 rows in pattern =
2" (5 cm).
To save time, take
time to check gauge.

+
ALTERNATIVE YARN CHOICE

Willow Yarns
Fawn Worsted

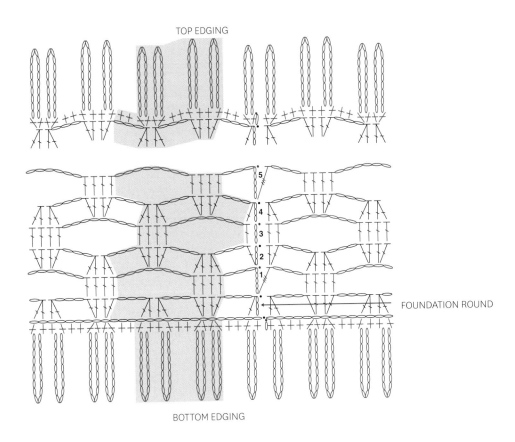

TOP EDGING

FOUNDATION ROUND

BOTTOM EDGING

COWL

Chain 338.

Being careful not to twist the chain, slip st in the first ch to form a ring.

Foundation Round (RS): Ch 3 (counts as dc here and throughout), dc in the next ch (counts as dc2tog), ch 3, skip the next 3 ch, *2 dc in each of the next 2 ch, ch 3, skip the next 3 ch, [dc2tog over the next 2 ch] twice, ch 3, skip the next 3 ch; repeat from the * around, ending with 2 dc in each of the next 2 ch, ch 3, skip the next 3 ch, dc2tog over the next 2 ch, join with a slip st in the top of the beginning ch-3.

Round 1: Ch 8, skip the next ch-3 sp, *dc in each of the next 4 dc, ch 8, skip the next ch-3 sp, skip the next 2 dc2tog, skip the next ch-3 sp; repeat from the * around, ending with dc in each of the next 4 dc, ch 3, dtr in the top of the beginning ch-3 in row below, join with a slip st in the 5th ch of the beginning ch-8.

Round 2: Ch 3, dc in the first st, ch 3, skip the next ch-3 sp, *[dc2tog over the next 2 dc] twice, ch 3, skip the next 3 ch, 2 dc in each of the next 2 ch, ch 3, skip the next 3 ch; repeat from the * around, ending with *[dc2tog over the next 2 dc] twice, ch 3, skip the next 3 ch, 2 dc in the fifth ch of the ch-8, join with a slip st to the top of the beginning ch-3.

Round 3: Ch 3, skip the first dc, dc in the next dc, *ch 8, skip the next ch-3 sp, skip the next 2 dc2tog, skip the next ch-3 sp, dc in each of the next 4 dc; repeat from the * around, ending with ch 8, skip the next ch-3 sp, skip the next 2 dc2tog, skip the next ch-3 sp, dc in each of the next 2 dc, join with a slip st to the top of the beginning ch-3.

Round 4: Ch 3, skip the first dc, dc in the next dc (counts as dc2tog), *ch 3, skip the next 3 ch, 2 dc in each of the next 2 ch, ch 3, skip the next 3 ch, [dc2tog over the next 2 dc] twice; repeat from the * around, ending with ch 3, skip the next 3 ch, 2 dc in each of the next 2 ch, ch 3, skip the next 3 ch, dc2tog over the next dc with the beginning ch-3, join with a slip st to the top of the beginning ch-3.

Repeat Rounds 1–4 twice. *Do not fasten off*.

TOP EDGING

Next Round (RS): Ch 1, (sc, ch 18, sc) in the same st as the last slip st, *2 sc in the next ch-3 sp, [sc in

the next dc, ch 18, sc in the next dc] twice, 2 sc in the next ch-3 sp, [sc, ch 18, sc] in each of the next 2 dc2tog; repeat from the * around, ending with 2 sc in the next ch-3 sp, [sc in the next dc, ch 18, sc in the next dc] twice, 2 sc in the next ch-3 sp, [sc, ch 18, sc] in the next dc2tog, join with a slip st in the top of the first sc.

Fasten off.

BOTTOM EDGING

Round 1: With RS facing, working across opposite side of foundation ch, join yarn with slip st in last ch at base of last st in Round 1, ch 1, sc in the same ch as the last slip st, ch 18, sc in the next ch, *2 sc in the next ch-3 sp, [sc, ch 18, sc] in each of the next 2 ch, 2 sc in the next ch-3 sp, [sc in the next dc, ch 18, sc in the next dc] twice; repeat from the * around, ending with 2 sc in the next ch-3 sp, [sc, ch 18, sc] in each of the next 2 ch, 2 sc in the next ch-3 sp, sc in the next ch, ch 18, sc in the next ch, join with a slip st in the top of the first sc.

Fasten off.

FINISHING

Weave in ends. Block to the finished measurements.

ORLAITHE

ARAN COWL

Keep warm and toasty in this cowl. Its textures are reminiscent of traditional knitted designs.

+

SIZE

One size

+

FINISHED MEASUREMENTS

9" (23 cm) deep × 22" (56 cm) in circumference

+

MATERIALS

• Plymouth Yarn *Worsted Merino Superwash* 4 (100% superwash merino wool; each approximately 3½ oz/ 100 g and 218 yd/ 199.5 m), 2 hanks of #70 Slate

• Crochet hook sizes G/6 (4 mm) and H/8 (5 mm) or sizes needed to obtain gauge

+

GAUGE

With larger hook, 16 sts and 14 rounds in pattern = 4" (10 cm). To save time, take time to check gauge.

+

ALTERNATIVE YARN CHOICE

Brown Sheep *Naturespun Worsted*

NOTES

- Although this project is worked in rounds, at the end of each round, join with a slip stitch to the beginning of the round, as indicated in the instructions. Ch 2 and turn.

- Always skip the hdc behind each FPst.

- Each FPtr, FPdc, and FPdtr counts as FPsts.

SPECIAL STITCHES

Popcorn = 5 dc in the indicated st; drop the loop from the hook; reinsert the hook in the first dc of the 5-dc group, pick up the dropped loop and pull it through the first dc (page 134).

Reverse Single Crochet (reverse sc) = Working from left to right, insert hook in next stitch, yarn over and pull up a loop; yarn over hook and draw loop through both loops on hook (page 135).

COWL

With the larger hook, chain 87.

Being careful not to twist the chain, make a slip st in the last ch to form a ring.

Foundation Round 1 (RS): Ch 2, skip the chain where the slip st was worked, *[dc in each of the next 2 ch, hdc in the next ch] 5 times, hdc in each of the next 4 ch, [dc in each of the next 2 ch, hdc in the next ch]

twice, hdc in each of the next 4 ch; repeat from the * around, ending with [dc in each of the next 2 ch, hdc in the next ch] 5 times, hdc in each of the next 4 ch, [dc in each of the next 2 ch, hdc in the next ch] twice, hdc in each of the next 3 ch, slip st in the top of the first ch-2, turn.

Foundation Round 2 (WS): Ch 2, skip the first st, hdc in each st around, ending with hdc in top of the first ch-2. Ch 2, turn.

Foundation Round 3: Ch 2, skip the hdc where the slip st was worked, *FPtr in each of the next 2 dc 2 rows below, skip 2 hdc after the last hdc made, hdc in the next hdc, skip the next 3 hdc, FPdtr in each of the next 2 dc 2 rows below, skip 2 hdc after the last hdc made, hdc in the next hdc, *working in front of the last 2 FPsts*, FPdtr in each of the 2 skipped dc 2 rows below, [skip 2 hdc after the last hdc made, hdc in the next hdc, FPtr in each of the next 2 dc 2 rows below] twice, skip 2 hdc after the last hdc made, hdc in each of the next 5 hdc, skip the next 3 hdc, FPdtr in each of the next 2 dc 2 rows below, skip 2 hdc after the last hdc made, hdc in the next hdc, *working in front of the last 2 FPsts*, FPdtr in each of the 2 skipped dc 2 rows below, skip 2 hdc after the last hdc made, hdc in each of the next 5 hdc; repeat from the * around, ending with FPtr in each of the next 2 dc 2 rows below, skip 2 hdc after the last

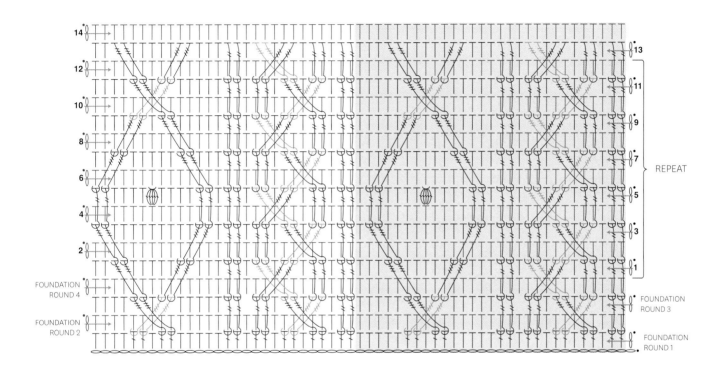

hdc made, hdc in the next hdc, skip the next 3 hdc, FPdtr in each of the next 2 dc 2 rows below, skip 2 hdc after the last hdc made, hdc in the next hdc, *working in front of the last 2 FPsts*, FPdtr in each of the 2 skipped dc 2 rows below, [skip 2 hdc after the last hdc made, hdc in the next hdc, FPtr in each of the next 2 dc 2 rows below] twice, skip 2 hdc after

the last hdc made, hdc in each of the next 5 hdc, skip the next 3 hdc, FPdtr in each of the next 2 dc 2 rows below, skip 2 hdc after the last hdc made, hdc in the next hdc, *working in front of the last 2 FPsts*, FPdtr in each of the 2 skipped dc 2 rows below, skip 2 hdc after the last hdc made, hdc in each of the next 4 hdc, slip st in the top of the first ch-2, turn.

Foundation Round 4: Repeat Foundation Round 2.

Round 1 (RS): Ch 2, skip the hdc where the slip st was worked, *[FPtr in each of the next 2 FPsts 2 rows below, skip 2 hdc after the last hdc made, hdc in the next hdc] twice, skip the next 3 hdc, FPdtr in each of the next 2 FPsts 2 rows below, skip 2 hdc after the last hdc made, hdc in the next hdc, *working behind the last 2 FPsts made*, FPdtr in each of the 2 skipped FPsts 2 rows below, skip 2 hdc after the last hdc made, hdc in the next hdc, FPtr in each of the next 2 FPsts 2 rows below, skip 2 hdc after the last hdc made, hdc in each of the next 3 hdc, skip the next 3 hdc, FPdtr in the next 2 FPsts 2 rows below, skip 2 hdc after the last hdc made, hdc in each of the next 5 hdc, FPdtr in the 2 skipped FPsts 2 rows below, skip 2 hdc after the last hdc made, hdc in each of the next 3 hdc; repeat from the * around, ending with [FPtr in each of the next 2 FPsts 2 rows below, skip 2 hdc after the last hdc made, hdc in the next hdc] twice, skip the next 3 hdc, FPdtr in each of the next 2 FPsts 2 rows below, skip 2 hdc after the last hdc made, hdc in the next hdc, *working behind the last 2 FPsts made*, FPdtr in each of the 2 skipped FPsts 2 rows below, skip 2 hdc after the last hdc made, hdc in the next hdc, FPtr in each of the next 2 FPsts 2 rows below, skip 2 hdc after the last hdc made, hdc in each of the next 3 hdc, skip the next

3 hdc, FPdtr in the next 2 FPsts 2 rows below, skip 2 hdc after the last hdc made, hdc in each of the next 5 hdc, FPdtr in the 2 skipped FPsts 2 rows below, skip 2 hdc after the last hdc made, hdc in each of the next 2 hdc, slip st in the top of the first ch-2, turn.

Round 2 and all WS rounds: Repeat Foundation Round 2.

Round 3: Ch 2, skip the hdc where the slip st was worked, *FPtr in each of the next 2 FPsts 2 rows below, skip 2 hdc after the last hdc made, hdc in the next hdc, skip the next 3 hdc, FPdtr in each of the next 2 FPsts 2 rows below, skip 2 hdc after the last hdc made, hdc in the next hdc, *working in front of the last 2 FPsts*, FPdtr in each of the 2 skipped dc 2 rows below, [skip 2 hdc after the last hdc made, hdc in the next hdc, FPtr in each of the next 2 FPsts 2 rows below] twice, skip 2 hdc after the last hdc made, hdc in the next hdc, skip the next 3 hdc, FPdtr in the next 2 FPsts 2 rows below, skip 2 hdc after the last hdc made, hdc in each of the next 9 hdc, FPdtr in the 2 skipped FPsts 2 rows below, skip 2 hdc after the last hdc made, hdc in the next hdc; repeat from the * around, ending with FPtr in each of the next 2 FPsts 2 rows below, skip 2 hdc after the last hdc made, hdc in the next hdc, skip the next 3 hdc, FPdtr in each of the next 2 FPsts 2 rows below, skip

2 hdc after the last hdc made, hdc in the next hdc, *working in front of the last 2 FPsts*, FPdtr in each of the 2 skipped dc 2 rows below, [skip 2 hdc after the last hdc made, hdc in the next hdc, FPtr in each of the next 2 FPsts 2 rows below] twice, skip 2 hdc after the last hdc made, hdc in the next hdc, skip the next 3 hdc, FPdtr in the next 2 FPsts 2 rows below, skip 2 hdc after the last hdc made, hdc in each of the next 9 hdc, FPdtr in the 2 skipped FPsts 2 rows below, slip st in the top of the first ch-2, turn.

Round 5: Ch 2, skip the hdc where the slip st was worked, *[FPtr in each of the next 2 FPsts 2 rows below, skip 2 hdc after the last hdc made, hdc in the next hdc] twice, skip the next 3 hdc, FPdtr in each of the next 2 FPsts 2 rows below, skip 2 hdc after the last hdc made, hdc in the next hdc, *working behind the last 2 FPsts made*, FPdtr in each of the 2 skipped FPsts 2 rows below, skip 2 hdc after the last hdc made, hdc in the next hdc, FPtr in each of the next 2 FPsts 2 rows below, skip 2 hdc after the last hdc made, hdc in the next hdc, FPtr in each of the next 2 FPsts 2 rows below, skip 2 hdc after the last hdc made, hdc in each of the next 4 hdc, Popcorn in the next hdc, hdc in each of the next 4 hdc, FPtr in each of the next 2 FPsts 2 rows below, skip 2 hdc after the last hdc made, hdc in the next hdc; repeat from the * around, ending with [FPtr in each of the next

2 FPsts 2 rows below, skip 2 hdc after the last hdc made, hdc in the next hdc] twice, skip the next 3 hdc, FPdtr in each of the next 2 FPsts 2 rows below, skip 2 hdc after the last hdc made, hdc in the next hdc, *working behind the last 2 FPsts made*, FPdtr in each of the 2 skipped FPsts 2 rows below, skip 2 hdc after the last hdc made, hdc in the next hdc, FPtr in each of the next 2 FPsts 2 rows below, skip 2 hdc after the last hdc made, hdc in the next hdc, FPtr in each of the next 2 FPsts 2 rows below, skip 2 hdc after the last hdc made, hdc in each of the next 4 hdc, Popcorn in the next hdc, hdc in each of the next 4 hdc, FPtr in each of the next 2 FPsts 2 rows below, slip st in the top of the first ch-2, turn.

Round 7: Ch 2, skip the hdc where the slip st was worked, *FPtr in each of the next 2 FPsts 2 rows below, skip 2 hdc after the last hdc made, hdc in the next hdc, skip the next 3 hdc, FPdtr in each of the next 2 FPsts 2 rows below, skip 2 hdc after the last hdc made, hdc in the next hdc, *working in front of the last 2 FPsts*, FPdtr in each of the 2 skipped dc 2 rows below, [skip 2 hdc after the last hdc made, hdc in the next hdc, FPtr in each of the next 2 FPsts 2 rows below] twice, skip 2 hdc after the last hdc made, hdc in each of the next 3 hdc, FPdtr in each of the 2 skipped FPsts 2 rows below, skip 2 hdc after the last hdc made, hdc in each of the next 5 hdc,

FPdtr in each of the next 2 FPsts 2 rows below, skip 2 hdc after the last hdc made, hdc in each of the next 3 hdc; repeat from the * around, ending with FPtr in each of the next 2 FPsts 2 rows below, skip 2 hdc after the last hdc made, hdc in the next hdc, skip the next 3 hdc, FPdtr in each of the next 2 FPsts 2 rows below, skip 2 hdc after the last hdc made, hdc in the next hdc, *working in front of the last 2 FPsts*, FPdtr in each of the 2 skipped dc 2 rows below, [skip 2 hdc after the last hdc made, hdc in the next hdc, FPtr in each of the next 2 FPsts 2 rows below] twice, skip 2 hdc after the last hdc made, hdc in each of the next 3 hdc, FPdtr in each of the 2 skipped FPsts 2 rows below, skip 2 hdc after the last hdc made, hdc in each of the next 5 hdc, FPdtr in each of the next 2 FPsts 2 rows below, skip 2 hdc after the last hdc made, hdc in each of the next 2 hdc, slip st in the top of the first ch-2, turn.

Round 9: Ch 2, skip the hdc where the slip st was worked, *[FPtr in each of the next 2 FPsts 2 rows below, skip 2 hdc after the last hdc made, hdc in the next hdc] twice, skip the next 3 hdc, FPdtr in each of the next 2 FPsts 2 rows below, skip 2 hdc after the last hdc made, hdc in the next hdc, *working behind the last 2 FPsts made*, FPdtr in each of the 2 skipped FPsts 2 rows below, skip 2 hdc after the last hdc made, hdc in the next hdc, FPtr in each of the next 2 FPsts 2 rows below, skip 2 hdc after the

last hdc made, hdc in each of the next 5 hdc, FPdtr in each of the 2 skipped FPsts 2 rows below, skip 2 hdc after the last hdc made, hdc in the next hdc, FPdtr in each of the next 2 FPsts 2 rows below, skip 2 hdc after the last hdc made, hdc in each of the next 5 hdc; repeat from the * around, ending with [FPtr in each of the next 2 FPsts 2 rows below, skip 2 hdc after the last hdc made, hdc in the next hdc] twice, skip the next 3 hdc, FPdtr in each of the next 2 FPsts 2 rows below, skip 2 hdc after the last hdc made, hdc in the next hdc, *working behind the last 2 FPsts made*, FPdtr in each of the 2 skipped FPsts 2 rows below, skip 2 hdc after the last hdc made, hdc in the next hdc, FPtr in each of the next 2 FPsts 2 rows below, skip 2 hdc after the last hdc made, hdc in each of the next 5 hdc, FPdtr in each of the 2 skipped FPsts 2 rows below, skip 2 hdc after the last hdc made, hdc in the next hdc, FPdtr in each of the next 2 FPsts 2 rows below, skip 2 hdc after the last hdc made, hdc in each of the next 4 hdc, slip st in the top of the first ch-2, turn.

Round 11: Ch 2, skip the hdc where the slip st is, *FPtr in each of the next 2 FPtr 2 rows below, skip 2 hdc after the last hdc made, hdc in the next hdc, skip the next 3 hdc, FPdtr in each of the next 2 FPsts 2 rows below, skip 2 hdc after the last hdc made, hdc in the next hdc, *working in front of the last 2*

FPsts, FPdtr in each of the 2 skipped FPsts 2 rows below, [skip 2 hdc after the last hdc made, hdc in the next hdc, FPtr in each of the next 2 FPsts 2 rows below] twice, skip 2 hdc after the last hdc made, hdc in each of the next 5 hdc, skip the next 3 hdc, FPdtr in each of the next 2 FPsts 2 rows below, skip 2 hdc after the last hdc made, hdc in the next hdc, *working in front of the last 2 FPsts*, FPdtr in each of the 2 skipped FPsts 2 rows below, skip 2 hdc after the last hdc made, hdc in each of the next 5 hdc; repeat from the * around, ending with FPtr in each of the next 2 FPtr 2 rows below, skip 2 hdc after the last hdc made, hdc in the next hdc, skip the next 3 hdc, FPdtr in each of the next 2 FPsts 2 rows below, skip 2 hdc after the last hdc made, hdc in the next hdc, *working in front of the last 2 FPsts*, FPdtr in each of the 2 skipped FPsts 2 rows below, [skip 2 hdc after the last hdc made, hdc in the next hdc, FPtr in each of the next 2 FPsts 2 rows below] twice, skip 2 hdc after the last hdc made, hdc in each of the next 5 hdc, skip the next 3 hdc, FPdtr in each of the next 2 FPsts 2 rows below, skip 2 hdc after the last hdc made, hdc in the next hdc, *working in front of the last 2 FPsts*, FPdtr in each of the 2 skipped FPsts 2 rows below, skip 2 hdc after the last hdc made, hdc in each of the next 4 hdc, slip st in the top of the first ch-2. Ch 2, turn.

Round 12: Repeat Foundation Row 2.

Repeat Rounds 1–12 once more. *Do not fasten off.* Change to the smaller hook, turn.

TOP EDGING

Round 1 (RS): Ch 1, sc in same st as slip st, sc in each st around, join with a slip st in the first sc, *do not turn*.

Round 2: Ch 1, reverse sc in each st (page 135) around, join with a slip st in the first sc.

Fasten off.

BOTTOM EDGING

For the edging on the second side, with the right side facing and the smaller hook, attach yarn with a slip st to the beginning of Foundation Round 1 and ch 1.

Round 1: With RS facing, working across opposite side of the foundation ch, join yarn in any ch, ch 1, sc in the same st as the slip st, sc in each ch around, join with a slip st to the first sc. *Do not turn.*

Round 2: Ch 1, reverse sc in each st around, join with a slip st in the first sc.

Fasten off.

Weave in ends.

SOLEIL

RAMIE SUMMER HAT

Made from the top down, this classic raffia hat will keep the sun off your face in style!

+
SIZE

One size

+
FINISHED MEASUREMENTS

Circumference:
21" (53.5 cm)
Height: 9" (23 cm)

+
MATERIALS

• Universal Yarn
Yashi
(4)
(100% raffia;
each approximately
1.41 oz/40 g and 99 yd/
90 m), 2 balls of
#107 Pewter

• Crochet hook size
H/8 (5 mm) or size
needed to obtain gauge

• Craft wire, 28 gauge,
1 yd (.9 m)

+
GAUGE

12 sts and 12 rounds
in pattern = 4" (10 cm).
To save time, take time
to check gauge.

+
ALTERNATIVE YARN CHOICE

Lily *Sugar 'n Cream*

SPECIAL STITCHES

Reverse Single Crochet (reverse sc) *Working from left to right*, insert hook in next stitch, yarn over, draw up a loop; yarn over hook and draw loop through both loops on hook (page 135).

HAT

Begin with an adjustable ring (page 129).

Round 1 (RS): Ch 1, 7 sc in the adjustable ring; join with a slip st in the top of the first sc—7 sc.

Round 2: Ch 1, *working in the back loop only*, 2 sc in each sc around; join with a slip st to the top of the first sc—14 sc.

Round 3: Ch 1, *working in the back loop only*, 2 sc in the next sc, sc in the next sc; repeat from the * around; join with a slip st to the top of the first sc—21 sc.

Round 4: Ch 1, *working in the back loop only*, 2 sc in the next sc, sc in each of the next 2 sc; repeat from the * around; join with a slip st to the top of the first sc—28 sc.

Round 5: Ch 1, *working in the back loop only*, 2 sc in the next sc, sc in each of the next 3 sc; repeat from the * around; join with a slip st to the top of the first sc—35 sc.

Round 6: Ch 1, *working in the back loop only*, 2 sc in the next sc, sc in each of the next 4 sc; repeat from the * around; join with a slip st to the top of the first sc—42 sc.

Round 7: Ch 1, *working in the back loop only*, 2 sc in the next sc, sc in each of the next 5 sc; repeat from the * around; join with a slip st to the top of the first sc—49 sc.

Round 8: Ch 1, *working in the back loop only*, 2 sc in the next sc, sc in each of the next 6 sc; repeat from the * around; join with a slip st to the top of the first sc—56 sc.

Round 9: Ch 1, *working in the back loop only*, 2 sc in the next sc, sc in each of the next 7 sc; repeat from the * around; join with a slip st to the top of the first sc—63 sc.

Rounds 10–20: Ch 1, *working in the back loop only*, sc in each sc around—63 sc.

Round 21: Ch 1, *working in the back loop only*, 2 sc in the next sc, sc in each of the next 6 sc; repeat from the * around; join with a slip st to the top of the first sc—72 sc.

Round 22: Ch 1, *working in the back loop only*, sc in each sc around—72 sc.

Round 23: Ch 1, *working in the back loop only*, 2 sc in the next sc, sc in each of the next 8 sc; repeat from the * around; join with a slip st to the top of the first sc—80 sc.

Round 24: Ch 1, *working in the back loop only*, 2 sc in the next sc, sc in each of the next 7 sc; repeat from the * around; join with a slip st to the top of the first sc—90 sc.

Round 25: Ch 1, *working in the back loop only*, 2 sc in the next sc, sc in each of the next 5 sc; repeat from the * around; join with a slip st to the top of the first sc—105 sc.

Lay the craft wire along the top of the last round worked.

Round 26: Ch 1, *working from left to right and working over the craft wire, enclosing it inside the crocheting*, reverse sc (page 135) in each sc around; join with a slip st in the top of the first reverse sc. Fasten off.

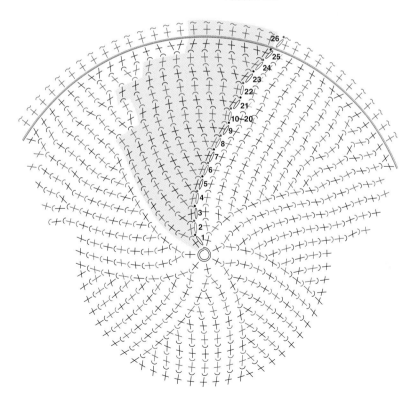

CHRISTIE

DIAGONAL HAT

This close-fitting cloche has the perfect amount of sparkle to ward off the cold with style. Made from the bottom up, it uses post stitches to create a swirl of texture.

+
FINISHED SIZE

8½" (21.5 cm) deep ×
17" (43 cm) in
circumference

+
MATERIALS

• Lion Brand *Wool-Ease Thick & Quick*
(79% acrylic/20% wool/
1% other fiber;
each approximately
5 oz /140 g and
92 yd/84 m),
1 ball of #304 Gemstone

• Crochet hook sizes
P/15 (11.5 mm)
and Q (16 mm)
or sizes needed
to obtain gauge

• Fiberfill stuffing,
optional

+
GAUGE

With the smaller hook,
17 sts and 4 rounds =
4" (10 cm). To save
time, take time to
check gauge.

+
ALTERNATIVE YARN CHOICE

Rowan *Cocoon*

SPECIAL STITCHES

Half double crochet 2 together (hdc2tog) = [Yarn over, insert the hook in the next st, yarn over, draw up a loop] twice, yarn over, draw through 5 loops on hook (page 131).

Single Crochet 2 Together (sc2tog) = [Insert the hook in next stitch and draw up a loop] twice, yarn over and draw through all 3 loops on hook (page 133).

HAT

With the larger hook, *loosely* chain 30. Being careful not to twist, join with a slip st to form a ring.

Round 1 (RS): Change to the smaller hook, ch 3, skip the st where the slip st was worked, dc in each ch around; join with a slip st to the top of the ch-3—30 dc.

Round 2: Ch 2 (counts as hdc here and throughout), skip the st where the slip st was worked, *FPdc in each of the next 2 sts, BPdc in each of the next 3 sts, FPdc in the next st; repeat from the * around, ending with FPdc in each of the next 2 sts, BPdc in each of the next 3 sts; join with a slip st in the top of the beginning ch-3.

Round 3: Ch 2, skip the st where the slip st was worked, *FPdc in each of the next 3 sts, BPdc in each of the next 3 sts; repeat from the * around, ending with FPdc in each of the next 3 sts, BPdc in each of the next 2 sts; join with a slip st in the top of the beginning ch-2.

Round 4: Ch 2, skip the st where the slip st was worked, *BPdc in the next st, FPdc in each of the next 3 sts, BPdc in each of the next 2 sts; repeat from the * around, ending with BPdc in the next st, FPdc in each of the next 3 sts, BPdc in the next st; join with a slip st in the top of the ch-2.

Round 5: Ch 2, skip the st where the slip st was worked, *BPdc in each of the next 2 sts, FPdc in each of the next 3 sts, BPdc in the next st; repeat from the * around, ending with BPdc in each of the next 2 sts, FPdc in each of the next 3 sts; join with a slip st in the top of the beginning ch-2.

Round 6: Ch 2, skip the st where the slip st was worked, *BPdc in each of the next 3 sts, FPdc in each of the next 3 sts; repeat from the * around, ending with BPdc in each of the next 3 sts, FPdc in each of the next 2 sts; join with a slip st in the top of the ch-2.

Round 7: Ch 2, skip the st where the slip st was worked, *FPdc in the next st, BPdc in each of the next 3 sts, FPdc in each of the next 2 sts; repeat from the * around, ending with FPdc in the next st, BPdc in each of the next 3 sts, FPdc in the next st; join with a slip st in the top of the ch-2.

Round 8 (Decrease Round): Ch 2, skip the st where the slip st was worked, *hdc2tog over the next 2 sts, hdc in the next st; repeat from the * around, ending with hdc2tog over the next 2 sts; join with a slip st to the top of the beginning ch-2—20 sts.

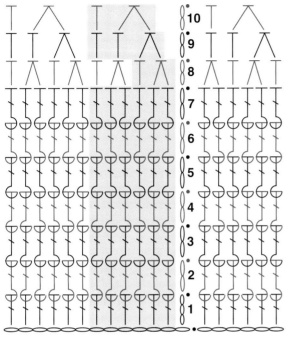

HAT

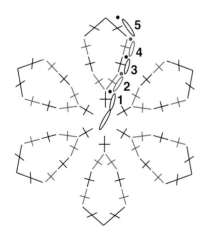

STUFFED TOPPER

Round 9: (Decrease Round): Ch 2, skip the st where the slip st was worked, *hdc2tog over the next 2 sts, hdc in each of the next 2 sts; repeat from the * around, ending with hdc2tog over the next 2 sts, hdc in the next st; join with a slip st to the top of the beginning ch-2—15 sts.

Round 10 (Decrease Round): Repeat Round 8—10 sts remain. Fasten off, leaving an 8" (20.5 cm) tail.

Thread the tail through the tops of the remaining 10 sts and pull tight to secure.

FINISHING

STUFFED TOPPER

With the larger hook, chain 2.

Round 1 (RS): Work 6 sc in second ch from the hook; join with a slip st in the first sc—6 sc.

Round 2: Ch 1, 2 sc in each sc around; join with a slip st to the first sc—12 sts.

Rounds 3 and 4: Ch 1, sc in each sc around; join with a slip st to the first sc—12 sts.

Round 5: Ch 1, *sc2tog over the next 2 sc; repeat from the * around; join with a slip st in the first st—6 sts. Fasten off, leaving an 8" (20.5 cm) tail.

Stuff yarn or optional fiberfill inside the ball.

Use the 8" (20.5 cm) tail to sew the stuffed ball onto the top of hat.

FENCHURCH

TOTE

Need to carry a day's worth of supplies? Stitch this handy tote bag. Plastic canvas hidden between the fabric and lining makes it sturdy but exceptionally lightweight.

+

SIZE

One size

+

FINISHED MEASUREMENTS

9½" (24 cm) wide ×
10" (25.5 cm) tall ×
4¼" (11 cm) deep

+

MATERIALS

• Universal Yarn
Deluxe Worsted
(4)
(100% wool; each
approximately 3.5 oz/
100 g and 219 yd/
200 m), 2 hanks of #12293
Burgundy (A), 1 hank of
#12173 Berry Crush (B),
and 1 hank of #71006
White Ash (C)

• Crochet hook sizes
G/6 (4 mm) and
H/8 (5 mm) or sizes
needed to obtain gauge

• Three 10½ × 13½"
(26.5 × 34.5 cm) sheets
of plastic canvas

• Matching fabric
for lining, approximately
½ yd (.46 m)

+

GAUGE

With the larger hook,
16 sts and 14 rows in body
pattern = 4" (10 cm).
To save time, take time
to check gauge.

+

**ALTERNATIVE
YARN CHOICE**

Coats & Clark
Red Heart With Love

- Throughout, each dc, reverse sc, and ch-3 counts as 1 stitch; each ch-1 at beginning of round *does not* count as a stitch.
- When making bottom and body of bag, RS is always facing you.
- Constructionwise, this tote bag is made in the round.

STRIPE PATTERN

Work in the following color sequence for sides: *One round each in A, B, A, C; repeat from the * for the pattern.

BOTTOM OF BAG

With the smaller hook and A, chain 21.

Round 1 (RS): Sc in the second ch from hook and in each of next 18 ch, 5 sc in last ch; *working in the unused loops of foundation ch*, sc in each of next 18 ch, 4 sc in last ch; join with a slip st to first sc—46 sts.

Round 2: Ch 1, sc in the same sc as the slip st, sc in each of the next 19 sc, 2 sc in each of next 3 sc, sc in each of the next 20 sc, 2 sc in each of next 3 sc; join with a slip st to the first sc—52 sts.

Round 3: Ch 1, sc in the same sc as the slip st, sc in each of the next 20 sc, [2 sc in the next sc, sc in the next sc] twice, 2 sc in the next sc, sc in each of the next 21 sc, [2 sc in the next sc, sc in the next sc] twice, 2 sc in the next sc; join with a slip st to first sc—58 sts.

Round 4: Ch 1, sc in the same sc as the slip st, sc in each of the next 21 sc, [2 sc in the next sc, sc in each of the next 2 sc] twice, 2 sc in next sc, sc in next 22 sc, [2 sc in the next sc, sc in each of the next 2 sc] twice, 2 sc in the next sc; join with a slip st to first sc—64 sts.

Round 5: Ch 1, sc in the same sc as the slip st, sc in each of the next 22 sc, [2 sc in the next sc, sc in each of the next 3 sc] twice, 2 sc in the next sc, sc in each of the next 23 sc, [2 sc in next sc, sc in each of the next 3 sc] twice, 2 sc in the next sc; join with a slip st to first sc—70 sts.

Round 6: Ch 1, sc in the same sc as the slip st, sc in each of the next 23 sc, [2 sc in the next sc, sc in each of the next 4 sc] twice, 2 sc in the next sc, sc in each of the next 24 sc, [2 sc in the next sc, sc in each of the next 4 sc] twice, 2 sc in the next sc; join with a slip st to first sc—76 sts.

Round 7: Ch 1, sc in the same sc as the slip st, sc in each of the next 24 sc, [2 sc in the next sc, sc in each of the next 5 sc] twice, 2 sc in the next sc, sc in each of the next 25 sc, [2 sc in the next sc, sc in each

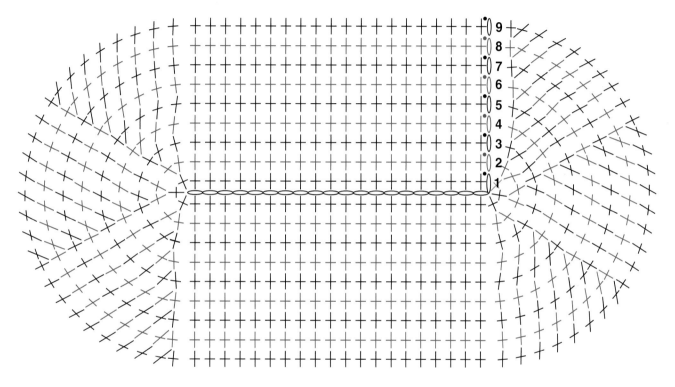

BOTTOM OF BAG

of the next 5 sc] twice, 2 sc in the next sc, sc in each of the next 4 sc; join with a slip st to first sc—82 sts.

Round 8: Ch 1, sc in the same sc as the slip st, sc in each of the next 25 sc, [2 sc in next sc, sc in each of the next 6 sc] twice, 2 sc in the next sc, sc in each of the next 26 sc, [2 sc in the next sc, sc in each of the next 6 sc] 3 times; join with a slip st to first sc—88 sts.

Round 9: Ch 1, sc in the same sc as the slip st, sc in each of the next 26 sc, [2 sc in the next sc, sc in each of the next 7 sc] twice, 2 sc in the next sc, sc in each of the next 27 sc, [2 sc in the next sc, sc in each of the next 7 sc] twice, 2 sc in the next sc; join with a slip st to first sc—94 sts.

BODY OF BAG

Round 1 (RS): *Working in the back loops only* (page 137), continue with Color A, ch 3, skip the first sc, dc in the next st and in each st around; join with a slip st to top of beginning ch-3—94 sts. Change to B.

Round 2: With B, ch 1, working from left to right *and in the front loops only* (page 137), reverse sc in each st around; join with a slip st to top of ch-3—82 sts. Change to A.

Round 3: With A, ch 3, skip the st where the slip st was worked, *working in the back loops only*, ch 3, dc in each st around, ending with a slip st to the top of ch-3—82 sts. Change to C.

Round 4: With C, repeat Round 2. Change to A.

Round 5: With A, repeat Round 3.

Rounds 6–36: Repeat Rounds 2–5 seven times; then repeat Rounds 2–4. Fasten off.

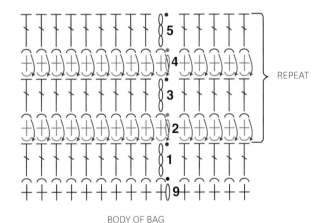

BODY OF BAG

FINISHING

BOTTOM TRIM

Round 1: With RS facing, join A with a slip st to unused loop of any st in Round 9 of Bottom of Bag and ch 1, slip st in each st around; join with a slip st to the first slip st. Fasten off.

Cut 1 piece of plastic canvas to fit in bottom of bag.

Cut 2 pieces of plastic canvas ½" (1.3 cm) less than height; overlap short edges by ½" (1.3 cm) and sew in a tube. Sew tube to bottom piece of plastic canvas.

Place assembled plastic canvas in bag and whip-stitch ½" (1.3 cm) below upper edge of bag on WS.

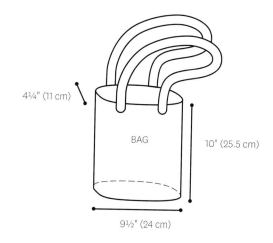

4¼" (11 cm)

BAG

10" (25.5 cm)

9½" (24 cm)

HANDLES *(make 4)*

With the smaller hook and A, chain 151.

Row 1 (RS): Sc in the second ch from hook and in each ch across, turn—150 sts.

Row 2: Ch 1, sc in each sc across. Fasten off.

With the wrong sides together, crochet two handles together to form a double-thick handle as follows: Join B with a slip st through both thicknesses at the beginning of the last row worked, and ch 1, working through double thickness, sc evenly around, working 3 sc in each corner; join with a slip st in first sc.

Fasten off.

Use whipstitch (page 139) to sew a strap onto each side of bag and plastic canvas as shown in photo, overlapping 2" (5 cm) on the RS of bag.

Using bottom of bag as a guide, cut lining fabric to fit, adding ½" (1.3 cm) all around.

Cut lining fabric to fit inside sides of bag, adding ½" (1.3 cm) all around for seam allowance. Sew bottom edge of lining to lining in bottom of the bag. Place lining in the bag, fold the top edge over, and whipstitch to the top of the bag, covering the plastic canvas.

GUINEVERE

LITTLE BAG WITH HANDLES

This clever and useful little bag features a simple textured pattern and awesome wooden handles. The easy-to-do lining ensures that keys and coins won't slip through the fabric.

+
SIZE
One size

+
FINISHED SIZE
Approximately 7½" (19 cm) wide × 8" (20.5 cm) tall, excluding handles

+
MATERIALS
• Brown Sheep *Lamb's Pride Worsted* **④** (85% wool/15% mohair; each approximately 4 oz/113 g and 190 yd/ 173 m), 1 skein of #M-77 Blue Magic

• Crochet hook size I/9 (5.5 mm) or size needed to obtain gauge

• Two Sunbelt Fasteners #SFPH-W17 wood purse handles in dark brown (3⅛" × 5¼" [8 × 13.5 cm])

• Coordinating fabric for lining, approximately 1 yd (.9 m)

+
GAUGE
13 sts and 12 rows in pattern = 4" (10 cm). To save time, take time to check gauge.

+
ALTERNATIVE YARN CHOICE
Coats & Clark *Red Heart Classic*

- This project is worked from the top down in two pieces.

FRONT OF BAG

Row 1 (RS): Join yarn with a slip st over one handle, ch 1, work 19 sc over handle (see opposite), turn—19 sc.

Row 2: Ch 1, [sc, tr] in the first sc, *sc in the next sc, tr in the next sc; repeat from the * 7 times, sc in the next sc, [tr, sc] in the last sc—21 sts, turn.

Row 3: Ch 1, sc in each st across, turn.

Row 4: Ch 1, 2 sc in first sc, *tr in the next sc, sc in the next sc; repeat from the * 8 times, tr in the next sc, 2 sc in the last sc—23 sts, turn.

Row 5: Repeat Row 3.

Row 6: Repeat Row 2—25 sts.

Row 7: Repeat Row 3.

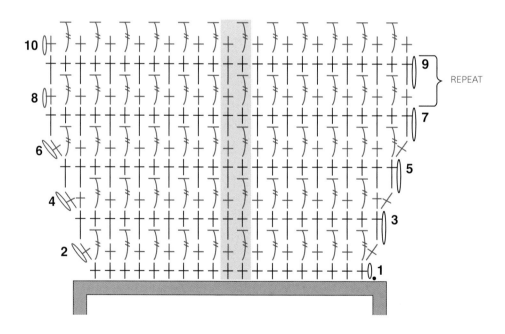

REPEAT

Row 8: Ch 1, sc in first sc, * tr in the next sc, sc in the next sc; repeat from the * across, turn.

Row 9: Repeat Row 3.

Repeat Rows 8 and 9 until the piece measures approximately 7½" (19 cm) from the bottom of the handle, ending with Row 9 of the pattern.

Fasten off.

BACK OF BAG

Work same as front of bag.

FINISHING

Use mattress stitch (page 139) to sew the sides and bottom of bag, leaving the upper 2" (5 cm) unsewn on both sides. Weave in ends.

LINING

Cut fabric to 15½" × 8½" (39.5 × 21.5 cm).

Fold in half to form a pocket, and sew in the bag, folding ¼" (6 mm) selvedge to the wrong side on all edges.

WORKING OVER THE HANDLE

Insert the hook under the handle, yarn over, draw up a loop, yarn over and draw through 2 loops on hook.

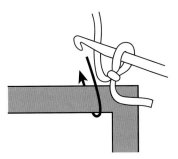

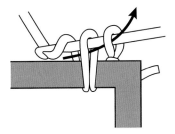

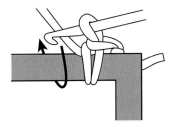

HARMONIA

FINGERLESS MITTS

You (or some lucky gift recipient) will love these fingerless mitts. Stitched in a simple openwork pattern, they are practical any time of the year.

+
SIZES

Small/Medium (Medium/Large, Large/1X, 1X/2X). Instructions are for the smallest size, with changes for other sizes noted in parentheses.

+
FINISHED MEASUREMENTS

11" (28 cm) long × 7 (7¾, 8½, 9¼)" (18 [19.5, 21.5, 23.5] cm) in circumference

+
MATERIALS

• Coats & Clark *Red Heart Boutique Unforgettable* (100% acrylic; each approximately 3.5 oz/100 g and 270 yd/247 m), 1 ball of #3932 Springtime

• Crochet hook size H/8 (5 mm) or size needed to obtain gauge

+
GAUGE

20 sts and 12 rows in pattern = 4" (10 cm). To save time, take time to check gauge.

+
ALTERNATIVE YARN CHOICE

Coats & Clark *Red Heart Soft*

MITTS *(make 2)*

Make a note of what color of the colorway you begin with, chain 36 (40, 44, 48). Join with a slip st to form a ring.

Round 1 (RS): Ch 1, sc in the same ch as the slip st, sc in the next ch, *ch 2, skip the next 2 ch, sc in each of the next 2 ch; repeat from the * around, ending with ch 2; join with a slip st to the top of the first sc—9 (10, 11, 12) ch-2 sps.

Round 2: Ch 3 (counts as dc here and throughout), skip the st where the last slip st was worked, dc in the next sc, *ch 2, skip the next ch-2 sp, dc in each of the next 2 sc; repeat from the * around, ending with ch 2; join with a slip st to the top of the beginning ch-3.

Round 3: Ch 1, sc in the same st as the slip st, sc in the next dc, *ch 2, skip the next ch-2 sp, sc in each of the next 2 dc; repeat from the * around, ending with ch 2; join with a slip st to the top of the first sc.

Rounds 4–21: Repeat Rounds 2 and 3 ten times.

Round 22 (thumbhole round): Ch 3, skip the st where the last slip st was worked, dc in the next sc, ch 2, skip the next ch-2 sp, dc in each of the next 2 sc, ch

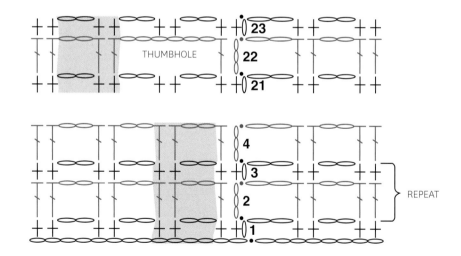

THUMBHOLE

REPEAT

6, skip the next ch-2 sp, skip the next 2 sc, skip the next ch-2 sp, *dc in each of the next 2 sc, ch 2, skip the next ch-2 sp; repeat from the * around; join with a slip st in the top of the beginning ch-3.

Round 23: Ch 1, sc in the same st as the slip st, sc in the next dc, ch 2, skip the next ch-2 sp, sc in each of the next 2 dc, ch 2, skip the next 2 ch, sc in each of the next 2 ch, skip the next 2 ch, *sc in each of the next 2 dc, ch 2, skip the next ch-2 sp; repeat from the * around; join with a slip st in the first sc.

Rounds 24–29: Repeat Rounds 2 and 3 six times.

Round 30: Ch 1, *skip the next 2 sc, [sc, dc, 2 tr, dc, sc] in the next ch-2 sp; repeat from the * around; join with a slip st to the first sc. Fasten off.

CUFF EDGING

With the RS facing, working across opposite side of foundation ch, join yarn with a slip st in any ch-2 sp, ch 1, *[sc, dc, 2 tr, dc, sc] in the ch-2 sp, skip the next 2 ch; repeat from the * around; join with a slip st in the first sc—9 (10, 11, 12) shells. Fasten off.

FINISHING

Weave in ends.

OOH LA LA

BERET

This winter warmer begins with a six-sided snowflake motif.
Stitch it, wear it, and show off your French fashionista side!

+
FINISHED SIZE

9" (23 cm) high ×
19½" (49.5 cm)
in circumference at
bottom edge;
28" (71 cm)
in circumference
at widest point

+
MATERIALS

• Universal Yarn
Amphora

(60% acrylic/20%
alpaca/20% mohair;
each approximately
3.5/100 g and 306 yd/
280 m), 1 ball of #102
Oxblood

• Crochet hook size
H/8 (5 mm)
crochet hook or
size needed to
obtain gauge

+
GAUGE

First 3 rounds =
3" (7.5 cm) in diameter.
14 sts and 9 rounds
in dc = 4" (10 cm).
To save time, take time
to check gauge.

+
**ALTERNATIVE
YARN CHOICE**

Classic Elite
Inca Alpaca

HAT

Make an adjustable ring (page 129).

Round 1 (RS): Ch 5 (counts as dc, ch 2 here and throughout), [dc, ch 2] 5 times in the adjustable ring; join with a slip st to the 3rd ch of the ch-5—6 ch-2 sps.

Round 2: Ch 5, dc in same st as the slip st, *ch 1, [dc, ch 2, dc] in the next dc; repeat from * around, ending with ch 1; join with a slip st in the 3rd ch of the beginning ch-5.

Round 3: Slip st in the next ch-2 sp, ch 3 (counts as dc here and throughout), [dc, ch 2, 2 dc] in the same ch-2 sp as the slip st, *ch 2, [2 dc, ch 2, 2 dc] in the next ch-2 sp; repeat from * around, ending with ch 2; join with a slip st to the top of the beginning ch-3.

Round 4: Slip st in the next dc, slip st in the next ch-2 sp, ch 3, [2 dc, ch 2, 3 dc] in the same ch-2 sp as the slip st, *ch 3, skip the next ch-2 sp, [3 dc, ch 2, 3 dc] in the next ch-2 sp; repeat from * around, ending with ch 3; join with a slip st in the top of the beginning ch-3.

Round 5: Slip st in each of the next 2 dc, slip st in the next ch-2 sp, ch 3, [3 dc, ch 2, 4 dc] in the same ch-2 sp as the slip st, *ch 4, [4 dc, ch 2, 4 dc] in the next ch-2 sp; repeat from the * around, ending with ch 4; join with a slip st in the top of the beginning ch-3.

Round 6: Slip st in each of the next 3 dc, slip st in the next ch-2 sp, ch 3, [3 dc, ch 2, 4 dc] in the same ch-2 sp as the slip st, *ch 4, sc in the next ch-4 sp, ch 4**, [4 dc, ch 2, 4 dc] in the next ch-2 sp; repeat from the * around, ending the last repeat at **; join with a slip st in the top of the ch-3.

Round 7: Slip st in each of the next 3 dc, slip st in the next ch-2 sp, ch 3, [3 dc, ch 2, 4 dc] in the same ch-2 sp as the slip st, *ch 4, [dc, ch 2, dc] in the next sc, ch 4**, [4 dc, ch 2, 4 dc] in the next ch-2 sp; repeat from the * around, ending with ch 4; join with a slip st in the top of the beginning ch-3.

Round 8: Slip st in each of the next 3 dc, slip st in the next ch-2 sp, ch 3, [3 dc, ch 2, 4 dc] in the same ch-2 sp as the slip st, *ch 4, [2 dc, ch 2, 2 dc] in the next ch-2 sp, ch 4**, [4 dc, ch 2, 4 dc] in the next ch-2 sp; repeat from the * around, ending last repeat at **; join with a slip st in the top of the beginning ch-3.

Round 9: Slip st in each of next 3 dc, slip st in next ch-2 sp, ch 1, sc in same st as the last slip st, *ch 4, dc in the next ch-4 sp, ch 4, dc in the next ch-2 sp, ch 4, dc in the next ch-4 sp, ch 4, sc in the next ch-2 sp; repeat from the * around, omitting last sc; join with a slip st to the top of the first sc.

Round 10: Ch 3, skip the st where the slip st was

worked, *[4 dc in the next ch-4 sp, dc in the next dc] 3 times, 4 dc in the next ch-4 sp, dc in the next sc; repeat from the * around, omitting the last dc; join with a slip st to the top of the ch-3—120 dc.

Rounds 11–15: Ch 3, skip the st where the slip st was worked, dc in each dc around; join with a slip st to the top of the ch-3.

Round 16: Ch 3, dc in the next dc, dc2tog over the next 2 dc, *dc in each of the next 2 dc, dc2tog over the next 2 dc; repeat from the * around; join with a slip st to the top of the beginning ch-3—90 sts.

Round 17: Ch 3, dc in the next st, dc2tog over the next 2 sts, *dc in each of the next 2 sts, dc2tog over the next 2 sts; repeat from the * around, ending with dc in each of last 2 sts; join with a slip st to the top of the beginning ch-3—68 sts.

Round 18: Ch 1, sc in each st around; join with a slip st in the top of the first sc—68 sc.

Rounds 19–21: Repeat Round 18. Fasten off.

FINISHING

Weave in ends.

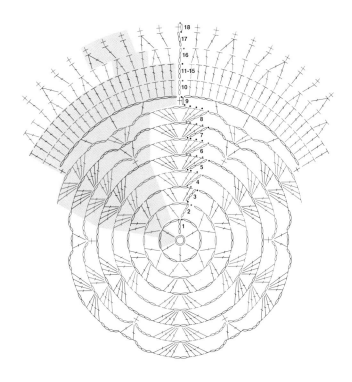

PREPSTER

BOA SCARF

Whip up this scarf in a single sitting. Made from super soft roving wool, it is soft and warm.

+

FINISHED SIZE

5" (12.5 cm) wide ×
88" (223.5 cm) long,
blocked

+

MATERIALS

• Plymouth Yarn
Galway Roving

(100% highland wool;
each approximately
3.5 oz/100 g and
54 yd/49.5 m),
2 balls of #754
Turtle Heather

• Crochet hook size P
(11.5 mm) or size needed
to obtain gauge

+

GAUGE

5 sts in pattern =
3" (7.5 cm).
To save time, take time
to check gauge.

+

ALTERNATIVE YARN CHOICE

Lion Brand *Wool-Ease
Thick & Quick*

SPECIAL STITCHES

Picot = Ch 3, slip st in 3rd ch from hook.

SCARF

Chain 138.

Row 1 (WS): Sc in the eighth ch from the hook, *ch 5, skip the next 5 ch, sc in next ch**, ch 4, skip the next 4 ch, sc in next ch; repeat from the * across, ending last repeat at **, ch 2, skip the next ch, dc in the last ch, turn—12 ch-5 sps; 12 ch-4 sps; one loop on each end, turn.

Row 2: Ch 1, sc in the first dc, skip the next ch-2 sp, *[5 dc, picot, 5 dc] in the next ch-5 sp, sc in the next ch-4 sp*; repeat from the * to * across, ending with [5 dc, picot, 5 dc] in the next ch-5 sp, skip the next 2 ch of end loop, sc in the next ch, [3 dc, picot, 3 dc] in same end loop, working across the opposite side of the Foundation Chain, sc in the same ch as the next sc, repeat from the * to * across, sc in ch at base of next sc. [3 dc, picot, 3 dc] in end loop; join with a slip st in the top of the first sc. Fasten off.

FINISHING

Weave in ends. Block to the finished measurements.

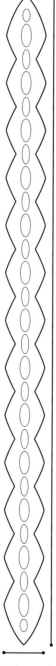

80" (203 cm)

5" (12.5 cm)

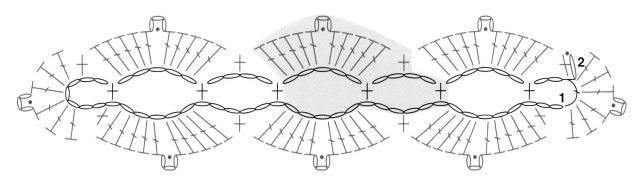

REDUCED SAMPLE OF PATTERN

DELICATA

REVERSIBLE WRAP

Light as air, this wrap is composed of an unusual stitch
pattern that looks great on both sides.

+
SIZE
One size

+
FINISHED MEASUREMENTS
27" (68.5 cm) deep × 70" (178 cm) long, blocked

+
MATERIALS
• Plymouth Yarn
Kid Gloss Hand Dyed

(72% super kid mohair/ 28% mulberry silk; each approximately .88 oz/25 g and 229 yd/209.5 m), 6 balls of #113 Blacks (A)

• Plymouth Yarn *Kid Gloss*

(72% super kid mohair/ 28% mulberry silk; each approximately .88 oz/25 g and 229 yd/209.5 m), 6 balls of #11 Chinchilla (B)

• Crochet hook size E/4 (3.5 mm) crochet hook or size needed to obtain gauge

• One stitch marker

+
GAUGE
24 sts and 20 rows in pattern = 4" (10 cm), blocked. To save time, take time to check gauge.

+
ALTERNATIVE YARN CHOICE
Lion Brand LB Collection *Silk Mohair*

NOTES

- This design is made sideways and uses 2 colors: A and B.
- This pattern is made of two interlocking layers of fabric, each a different color.
- Each row is worked in the stitches or spaces on the last row of the same color. You will never be working A in a stitch or space worked with B.

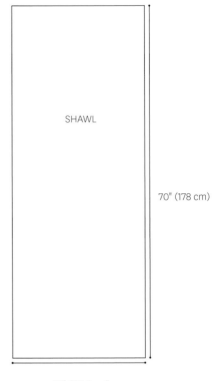

SHAWL

70" (178 cm)

27" (68.5 cm)

WRAP

With A, chain 425.

Place a marker in the eight ch from the hook.

Foundation Row 1 (RS): Dc in the tenth ch from the hook, dc in the next ch, *ch 3, skip the next 3 ch, dc in each of the next 2 ch; repeat from the * across, ending with ch 3, skip the next 3 ch, dc in the last ch. Remove the loop from the hook, and make it large so it doesn't unravel. *Do not turn.*

Foundation Row 2 (RS): *Working in front of the last row*, join B with a slip st to the eighth ch (the marked ch), ch 6, *working behind the last row* (page 136), dc in the same ch as where the slip st was made, *working behind the last row*, dc in the center ch of the next ch-3 of the Foundation Ch, ch 3, **working in front of the last row* (page 136), dc in the same ch of the Foundation Ch as the last dc made, *working in front of the last row*, dc in the center ch of the next ch-3 of the Foundation Ch, ch 3, *working behind the last row*, dc in the same ch of the Foundation Ch as the last dc, *working behind the last row*, dc in the center ch of the next ch-3 of the Foundation Ch, ch 3; repeat from the * across, ending with *working in front of the last row*, dc in the same ch of the Foundation ch as the last dc. Remove the loop from the hook, and make it large so it doesn't unravel.

Row 1 (WS): Place the A loop back onto the hook, ch 6, turn. *Working behind the last B row*, dc in each of the next 2 dc worked with A, ch 3, *working in front of the last B row, dc in each of the next 2 dc worked with A, ch 3, working behind the last B row, dc in each of the next 2 dc worked with A, ch 3*; repeat from the * across, ending with *working in front of the last B row*, dc in the last ch-sp of the previous

A row. Remove the loop from the hook, and make it large so it doesn't unravel. *Do not turn.*

Row 2 (WS): *Keeping the loop in front of the last A row*, place the B loop back onto the hook and ch 6, *working in front of the last A row*, dc in the first ch-3 sp of the previous row worked with B, *working in front of the last A row*, dc in the next ch-3 sp on the previous B row, ch 3, **working behind the last A row*, dc in the same ch-3 sp as the last dc made, working behind the last A row*, dc in the next ch-3 sp of the previous B row, ch 3, *working in front of the

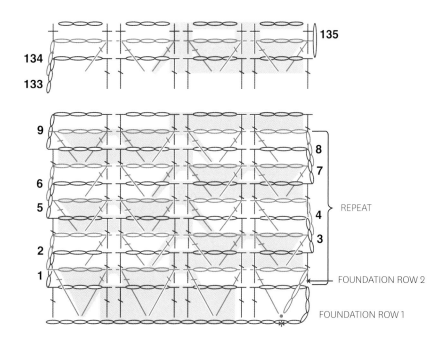

last A row, dc in the same sp as the last dc made, working in front of the last A row, dc in the next ch-3 sp on the previous B row, ch 3; repeat from the * across, ending with working behind the last A row, dc in the same sp as the last dc on previous B row. Remove the loop from the hook, and make it large so it doesn't unravel.

Row 3 (RS): Place the A loop back onto the hook, ch 6, turn. Working in front of the last B row, dc in each of the next 2 dc worked with A, ch 3, *working in behind the last B row, dc in each of the next 2 dc worked with A, ch 3, working in front of the last B row, dc in each of the next 2 dc worked with A, ch 3; repeat from the * across, ending with working behind the last B row, dc in the last ch-sp of the previous A row. Remove the loop from the hook, and make it large so it doesn't unravel. Do not turn.

Row 4 (RS): Repeat Row 2.

Row 5 (WS): Repeat Row 3.

Row 6 (WS): Keeping the loop in front of the last A row, place the B loop back onto the hook and ch 6, working behind the last A row, dc in the first ch-3 sp of the previous row worked with B, working behind the last A row, dc in the next ch-3 sp on the previous B row, ch 3, *working in front of the last A row, dc in the same ch-3 sp as the last dc made, working

in front of the last A row, dc in the next ch-3 sp of the previous B row, ch 3, working behind the last A row, dc in the same sp as the last dc made, working behind the last A row, dc in the next ch-3 sp on the previous B row, ch 3; repeat from the * across, ending with working in front of the last A row, dc in the same ch-sp as the last dc on previous B row. Remove the loop from the hook, and make it large so it doesn't unravel.

Row 7 (RS): Repeat Row 1.

Row 8 (RS): Repeat Row 6.

Rows 9–134: Repeat Rows 1–8 (15 times); then repeat Rows 1–6.

Row 135 (RS): Place A back onto the hook, ch 1, working behind the last B row, sc in the first dc on the previous A row, ch 3, working in front of the last B row, sc in each of the next 2 dc on the previous A row, ch 3, *working behind the last B row, sc in each of the next 2 dc on the previous A row, ch 3, working in front of the last B row, sc in each of the next 2 dc on the previous A row, ch 3; repeat from the * across, ending with working in behind the last B row, sc in the last ch-3 sp. Fasten off.

FINISHING

Weave in ends. Block to the finished measurements.

ASTRID

TRIANGULAR SHAWL

Choose your favorite colors for this useful wardrobe piece because you'll want to wear it often. Made from the top down with shell stitches, its size is easily customizable!

+

SIZE

One size

+

FINISHED SIZE

54" (137 cm) wide ×
28" (171 cm), blocked

+

MATERIALS

• Cascade
Heritage Silk
🄵
(85% superwash wool/
15% mulberry silk;
each approximately
3½ oz/100 g and
437 yd/400 m),
1 hank each of #5660
Gray (A), #5686 China
Blue (B), and #5711
Chalk Violet (C)

• Crochet hook size
H/8 (5 mm) or size
needed to obtain gauge

• One open ring
stitch marker

+

GAUGE

3 pattern repeats and
10 rows in pattern =
4" (10 cm), blocked.
To save time, take time
to check gauge.

+

ALTERNATIVE YARN CHOICE

Berroco Ultra
Alpaca Light

SPECIAL STITCHES

Picot = Ch 3, slip st in 3rd ch from hook.

COLOR SEQUENCE

Work in the following color sequence throughout:
*2 rows each of A, B, C; repeat from the * for the pattern.

SHAWL

Begin with an adjustable ring (page 129).

Row 1 (WS): With A, ch 6 (counts as tr, ch-2 here and throughout), [dc, ch 2, dc] 3 times in the adjustable ring, ch 2, tr in the adjustable ring, turn.

Row 2: Ch 6, skip the first ch-2 sp, 5 dc in the next ch-2 sp, [sc, ch 3, sc] in the next ch-2 sp, 5 dc in the next ch-2 sp, ch 2, tr under the turning-ch, turn. Change to B.

Row 3: With B, ch 6, [dc, ch 2, dc] in the first ch-2 sp, skip the next 2 dc, [dc, ch 2, dc] *in the front loop only* (page 135) of the next dc, [dc, ch 2, dc] 3 times in the next ch-3 sp, skip the next 2 dc, [dc, ch 2, dc] *in the front loop only* of the next dc, [dc, ch 2, dc, ch 2, tr] under the turning-ch, turn.

Row 4: Ch 6, skip the first ch-2 sp, 5 dc in the next ch-2 sp, sc in the next ch-2 sp, 5 dc in the next ch-2 sp, [sc, ch 3, sc] in the next ch-2 sp, 5 dc in the next ch-2 sp, sc in the next ch-2 sp, 5 dc in the next ch-2 sp, ch 2, tr under the turning-ch, turn. Change to C.

Row 5: With C, ch 6, [dc, ch 2, dc] in the first ch-2 sp, skip the next 2 dc, [dc, ch 2, dc] *in the front loop only* of the next dc, [dc, ch 2, dc] in the next sc, skip the next 2 dc, [dc, ch 2, dc] *in the front loop only* of the next dc, [dc, ch 2, dc] 3 times in the next ch-3 sp, skip the next 2 dc, [dc, ch 2, dc] *in the front loop only* of the next dc, [dc, ch 2, dc] in the next sc, skip the next 2 dc, [dc, ch 2, dc] *in the front loop only* of the next dc, [dc, ch 2, dc, ch 2, tr] under the turning-ch, turn.

Row 6: Ch 6, skip the first ch-2 sp, [5 dc in the next ch-2 sp, sc in the next ch-2 sp] twice, 5 dc in the next ch-2 sp, [sc, ch 3, sc] in the next ch-2 sp, place marker in ch-3 sp just made, [5 dc in the next ch-2 sp, sc in the next ch-2 sp] twice, 5 dc in the next ch-2 sp, ch 2, tr under the turning-ch, turn. Change to A. Move marker up as work progresses.

Row 7: With A, ch 6, [dc, ch 2, dc] in the first ch-2 sp, *skip the next 2 dc, [dc, ch 2, dc] in the front loop only of the next dc, [dc, ch 2, dc] in the next sc*; repeat from * to * across to last shell before marked ch-3 sp, skip the next 2 dc, [dc, ch 2, dc] *in the front loop only* of the next dc, [dc, ch 2, dc] 3 times in the next marked ch-3 sp, repeat from * to * across to last shell, skip the next 2 dc, [dc, ch 2, dc]

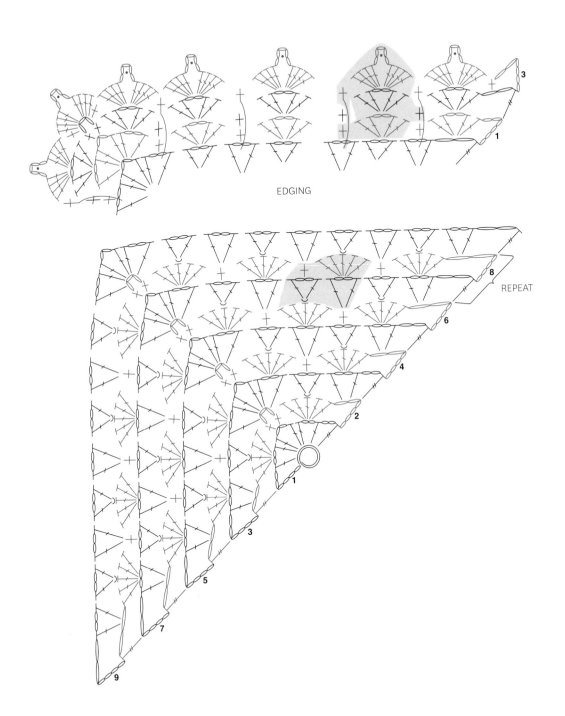

EDGING

REPEAT

in the front loop only of the next dc, [dc, ch 2, dc, ch 2, tr] under the turning-ch, turn.

Row 8: Ch 6, skip the first ch-2 sp, *5 dc in the next ch-2 sp, sc in the next ch-2 sp*; repeat from * to * across to ch-2 sp before next marker, 5 dc in the next ch-2 sp, [sc, ch 3, sc] in the next marked ch-2 sp, repeat from * to * across to last 2 ch-2 sps, 5 dc in the next ch-2 sp, ch 2, tr under the turning-ch, turn. Change to B.

Rows 9–52: Repeat Rows 7 and 8 twenty-two times, working in the following color sequence: *2 rows each of B, C, A; repeat from * throughout. *Do not fasten off*.

EDGING

Row 1 (RS): Ch 6, *[2 dc, ch 2, 2 dc] in the next ch-2 sp, sc in the next ch-2 sp*; repeat from the * to * across to marked ch-3 sp, work [dc, ch 2, dc] 3 times in the marked ch-3 sp, sc in the next ch-2 sp, then repeat from the * to * across to last ch-2 sp, [2 dc, ch 2, 2 dc, ch 2, tr] under the turning-ch, turn.

Row 2: Ch 6, skip the first ch-2 sp, *[2 dc, ch 2, 2 dc] in the next ch-2 sp, sc in the next sc*; repeat from the * to * across to marked ch-3 sp, work [sc, ch 3, sc] in the marked ch-2 sp, repeat from the * to * across to last ch-2 sp, ch 2, tr under the turning-ch, turn.

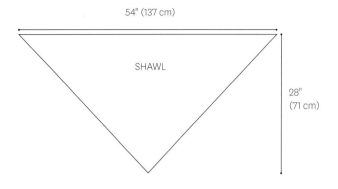

54" (137 cm)

SHAWL

28" (71 cm)

Row 3: Ch 6, sc in the first ch-2 sp, *[4 dc, ch 4, slip st in the third ch from the hook, ch 1, 4 dc] in the next ch-2 sp, sc in the next ch-2 sp 3 rows below*; repeat from the * to * across to ch-2 sp before marked ch-3 sp, [4 dc, ch 4, slip st in the third ch from the hook, ch 1, 4 dc] in the next ch-2 sp, [sc, 4 dc, ch 1, picot, ch 1, 4 dc, sc] in the marked ch-3 sp, repeat from the * to *across, to last ch-2 sp of shell, [4 dc, ch 4, slip st in the third ch from the hook, ch 1, 4 dc] in the next ch-2 sp, [sc, ch 2, tr] under the turning-ch. Fasten off.

FINISHING

Weave in ends. Block to the finished measurements.

PHOEBE

RING

Crochet this pretty ring in no time! Jump rings, readily available at any crafts store, provide the bling.

+
SIZE
One size

+
**FINISHED
MEASUREMENTS**
Ring face measures
1⅛" (29 mm) ×
1½" (38 mm)

+
MATERIALS
• Universal Yarn
Garden 10
(100% Egyptian
mercerized cotton;
each approximately
1.75 oz/50 g and
136 yd/125 m), 1 ball
of #700-54 Caramel

• 3 Jump rings,
12 mm (Darice *Chain
Maille Rings* were used
in sample project)

• Crochet hook size
7 (1.65 mm) or size
needed to obtain gauge

• 2 Open ring
stitch markers

+
GAUGE
Approximately
5 sts = ½" (1.3 cm).
Gauge is not crucial
to the success of
this project.

+
**ALTERNATIVE
YARN CHOICE**
Coats & Clark Aunt Lydia's
*Classic Cotton Crochet
Thread*, Size 10

NOTES

- Close the jump rings tightly with your fingers. A nail file may be used to smooth out edges of the join, if necessary.

- The ring size can be adjusted by changing the number of chains made for the band.

RING

Round 1 (RS): Join thread with a slip st around the first jump ring, ch 1, work 12 sc around the first jump ring; work 6 sc around the second jump ring; work 12 sc around third jump ring; work 6 sc around the opposite side of the second jump ring, join with a slip st in the first sc on the first jump ring—36 sc.

Round 2: Ch 1, *working around the first ring*, sc in the same st as the last slip st, ch 2, skip the next st, sc in each of the next 3 sts, ch 3, skip the next 2 sts, sc in each of the next 3 sts, ch 2, skip the next st, sc in the last st; *working around the first side of the second ring*, skip the first st, sc in the next st, ch 3, skip the next 2 sts, sc in the next st, skip the last sc; *working around the third ring*, sc in the first st, ch 2, skip the next st, sc in each of the next 3 sts, ch 3, skip the next 2 sts, sc in each of the next 3 sts, ch 2, skip the next st, sc in the next st; *working on opposite side of the second ring*, skip the first st, sc in the next st, ch 3, skip the next 2 sts, sc in the next

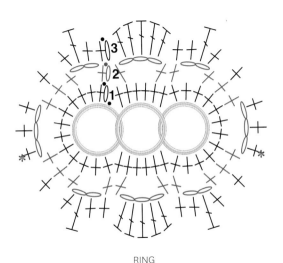

RING

st, skip the last st, join with a slip st in the first sc on the first ring.

Round 3: Ch 1, *working around the first ring*, sc in the same st as the last slip st, [sc, dc, sc] in the next ch-2 sp, skip the next st, sc in the next st, skip the next st, 3 sc in the next ch-3 sp, place a split ring marker in this last sc made, skip the next st, sc in the next st, skip the next st, [sc, dc, sc] in the next ch-2 sp, sc in the next st; *working around the first side of the second ring*, work 5 dc in the ch-3 sp, *working around the third ring*, [sc, dc, sc] in the next ch-2 sp, skip the next st, sc in the next st, skip the next st, 3 sc in the next ch-3 sp, place a split ring marker in the first of the last 3 sc made, skip the next st, sc in the next st, skip the next st, [sc,

dc, sc] in the next ch-2 sp, sc in the next st; *working around the opposite side of the second ring*, 5 dc in the ch-3 sp, join with a slip st in the first sc. Fasten off.

BAND

With the right side facing, join thread with a slip st in the first marked st, ch 10, join with a slip st to the marked st on the opposite side, slip st in the next st on the same side as the last slip st, ch 10, slip st in the next st on the opposite side, slip st in the next st on the same side as the last slip st, ch 4, work sc over both ch-10 spaces to join them, ch 5, join with a slip st to the next st on the opposite side. Fasten off.

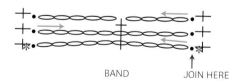

BAND   JOIN HERE

DANELLE

BRACELET

Add some bling to your wrist! Super silky yarn makes this bracelet comfortable to wear.

+

SIZE

One size

+

FINISHED MEASUREMENTS

Approximately 1½" (4 cm) × 8" (20.5 cm)

+

MATERIALS

• Patons *Metallic* (63% nylon/28% acrylic/ 9% wool; each approximately 3 oz/ 85 g and 251 yd/230 m), 1 ball of #95201 Metallic Teal

• Crochet hook size D/3 (3.25 mm) or size needed to obtain gauge

• 74 Size 4/0 beads (Beader's Paradise 4/0 Czech glass beads in crystal with silver lining were used on the sample project)

• One dental floss threader to string beads onto yarn

+

GAUGE

5 sts and 4 rows in pattern = ¾" (2 cm). To save time, take time to check gauge.

+

ALTERNATIVE YARN CHOICE

Coats & Clark Red Heart *Sparkle Soft*

NOTE • Unless stated otherwise, all stitches are worked *in the back loop only* (page 137).

SPECIAL STITCHES

Single crochet 2 together (sc2tog) = [Insert the hook in the next st and pull up a loop] twice, yarn over the hook and draw it through all 3 loops on the hook (page 133).

Beaded chain (Bch) = Slide a bead up close to the last st made, yarn over, draw yarn through loop (page 133).

BRACELET

FIRST BAND

String 32 beads onto the working yarn.

Chain 6.

Foundation Row (RS): Sc in the second ch from hook and in each ch across, turn—5 sc.

Row 1 (WS): Ch 3, (counts as dc here and throughout), skip the first sc, dc in the next st, hdc in the next st, sc in the next st, slip st in the next st, turn—5 sts.

Row 2: Ch 1, sc2tog worked across the first 2 sts, sc in each of the next 2 sts, 2 sc in the last st, turn—5 sts.

Row 3: Ch 1, 2 sc in the first sc, sc in each of the next 2 sts, sc2tog worked across the last 2 sts, turn—5 sts.

Rows 4–8: Repeat Rows 2 and 3 twice, then repeat Row 2 once.

Row 9: Ch 1, [sc, Bch, sc] in the first st, [Bch, sc in the next st] twice, Bch, sc2tog over the next 2 sts, turn—4 Bch.

Row 10: Ch 1, sc2tog worked across the first 2 sts, [skip the next ch-1 sp, sc in the next st] twice, 2 sc in the last sc, turn.

Rows 11–24: Repeat Rows 9 and 10 seven times, for a total of 8 beaded rows, turn.

Row 25: Repeat Row 3.

Rows 26–28: Work as Rows 2–3 once; then repeat Row 2 once.

Row 29: Ch 1, 2 sc in the first st, sc in each of the next 2 sts, sc2tog worked across the last 2 sts, turn.

Row 30: Ch 3, skip the first st, dc in the next st, hdc in the next st, sc in the next st, slip st in the last st, turn.

Row 31: Ch 1, sc in each st across. Fasten off.

SECOND BAND

String 32 beads onto the working yarn.

Chain 6.

Foundation Row (RS): Sc in the second ch from hook and in each ch across, turn—5 sc.

Row 1 (WS): Ch 1, slip st in the first st, sc in next st, hdc in the next st, dc in the next st, tr in the last st, turn—5 sts.

Row 2: Ch 1, 2 sc in the first st, sc in each of the next 2 sts, sc2tog worked across the last 2 sts, turn.

Row 3: Ch 1, sc2tog worked across the first 2 sts, sc in each of the next 2 sts, 2 sc in the last st, turn—5 sts.

Rows 4–8: Repeat Rows 2–3 twice; then repeat Row 2 once.

Row 9: Ch 1, sc2tog worked across the first 2 sts, [Bch, sc in the next st] twice, [Bch, sc, Bch, sc] in the last sc, turn—4 Bch.

Row 10: Ch 1, 2 sc in the first st, [skip the Bch, sc in the next sc] twice, sc2tog worked across the last 2 sts, turn.

Rows 11–24: Repeat Rows 9 and 10 seven times for a total of 8 beaded rows.

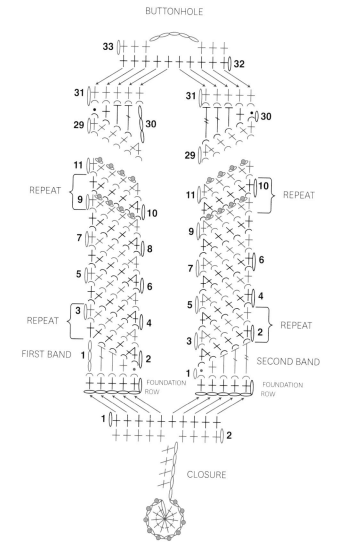

BUTTONHOLE

FIRST BAND

SECOND BAND

FOUNDATION ROW

CLOSURE

REPEAT

Row 26–29: Repeat Row 2 and 3 twice.

Row 30: Ch 1, slip st in the first st, sc in the next st, hdc in the next st, dc in the next st, tr in the last st, turn.

Row 31: Ch 1, sc in each st across, turn. *Do not fasten off.*

BUTTON HOLE EDGING

For the remaining rows, work through both front and back loops.

Row 32: Ch 1, sc in each st across Second Band, then with the right side of the First Band facing, sc in each sc across Row 31 of the First Band, turn.

Row 33: Ch 1, sc in each of the first 3 sts, ch 5, skip the next 4 sts, sc in each of the last 3 sts. Fasten off.

BUTTON EDGING

Row 1 (RS): String 10 beads onto the working yarn, working across opposite side of Foundation Ch, join yarn with a slip st in first ch in Foundation Ch of the First Band, ch 1, sc in each ch across the side edge of the band, with RS of Second Band facing, sc in each ch across the side edge of the Second Band, turn.

Row 2: Ch 1, sc in each of the first 4 sts, ch 5, work 10 Bch, ch 1, turn, yarn over, draw up a loop in each of the last 10 Bch sts just made, yarn over, draw through all 11 loops on the hook (sc10tog made); skip the next ch, sc in each of the last 4 ch; skip the next sc on the band, sc in each of the last 5 sts. Fasten off.

FINISHING

Weave in ends.

HAYMARKET

BIAS SCARF

Worked on the bias, this scarf is easy to stitch.

Choose your favorite colors and off you go!

+
SIZE
One size

+
FINISHED SIZE
7½" (19 cm) × 70" (178 cm)

+
MATERIALS
• Cascade *Venezia* Sport
(70% merino wool/ 30% silk; each approximately 3½ oz/100 g and 307.5 yd/281 m), 1 hank each of #190 Chocolate (A), #199 Shitake (B), and #132 Mouse (C)

• Crochet hook size H/8 (5 mm) or size needed to obtain gauge

+
GAUGE
14 dc and 9 rows = 4" (10 cm).
To save time, take time to check gauge.

+
ALTERNATIVE YARN CHOICE
Brown Sheep Yarn Company *Naturespun Sport*

COLOR SEQUENCE

Work in the following color sequence: *2 rows each of A, B, C, B; repeat from the * throughout.

SCARF

With A, chain 39.

Foundation Row (RS): Dc in the fourth ch from the hook, 2 dc in the next ch, dc in each of the next 30 ch, [dc2tog over next 2 ch] twice, turn—36 sts.

Row 1 (WS): Ch 3 (counts as dc here and throughout), skip the first dc2tog (counts as dc2tog), dc in the next dc2tog, dc in each of the next 30 dc, 2 dc in the next dc, 2 dc in the top of the turning-ch-3, turn.

Row 2: Ch 3, dc in the first dc, 2 dc in the next dc, dc in each of the next 30 dc, [dc2tog over next 2 sts] twice, turn.

Repeat Rows 1 and 2 until the piece measures approximately 67" (1.7 m) from the beginning, ending with 2 rows of A, then repeat Row 1. *Do not fasten off.*

FINISHING

Edging: With A, ch 2, hdc evenly around, working 3 hdc in each corner; join with a slip st in top of the beginning ch-2. Fasten off.

Weave in ends. Block to the finished measurements.

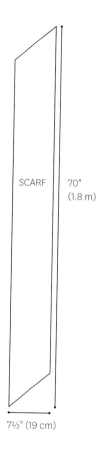

SCARF   70" (1.8 m)

7½" (19 cm)

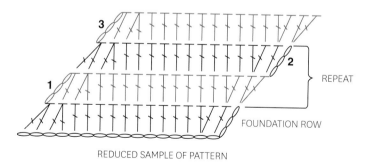

REDUCED SAMPLE OF PATTERN

LOUISA

MARKET BAG

Help keep our glorious planet green by switching to a durable and reuseable market bag. This design has the perfect amount of openwork and solid stitching, so none of your purchased goodies will poke through the sides!

+

SIZE

One size

+

**FINISHED
MEASUREMENTS**

22" (56 cm) long
including handles;
27" (68.5 cm)
in circumference.

+

MATERIALS

• Plymouth Yarn
Linen Concerto
3
(48% rayon/42% linen/
10% cotton;
each approximately
1.75 oz/50 g and
101 yd/92.5 m),
3 balls of #05
Heather Rose

• Crochet hook size
H/8 (5 mm) or size
needed to obtain gauge

+

GAUGE

15 dc and 8 rounds
in pattern = 4" (10 cm).
To save time, take time
to check gauge.

+

**ALTERNATIVE
YARN CHOICE**

Univeral Yarn Fibra
Natura Flax

NOTES
- Each dc, ch-1 space, and beginning ch-3 counts as a stitch; each beginning ch-4 *counts as 2 stitches*.
- When making the bottom and body of bag, the right side is always facing.

SPECIAL STITCHES

Double crochet 2 together (dc2tog) = Yarn over, insert the hook in the next st and pull up a loop; yarn over and draw yarn through 2 loops on hook, yarn over; insert the hook in the next st and pull up a loop, yarn over and draw yarn through 2 loops on hook, yarn over, draw through 3 loops on hook (page 134).

Double crochet 3 together (dc3tog) = Yarn over, insert the hook in next st and pull up a loop (3 loops are on your hook); yarn over and draw through 2 loops on the hook; [yarn over, insert hook in next st and pull up a loop; yarn over and draw it through 2 loops on the hook] twice, yarn over the hook and draw loop through all 4 loops on hook (page 134).

BOTTOM OF BAG

Begin with an adjustable ring (page 129).

Round 1 (RS): Ch 3 (counts as the dc here and throughout), 11 dc in the adjustable ring, join with a slip st in top of beginning ch-3—12 dc.

Round 2: Ch 4 (counts as a dc, ch 1 here and throughout), [dc, ch 1] in each dc around; join with a slip st in 3rd ch of the beginning ch-4—12 dc and 12 ch-1 sps.

Round 3: Ch 3, dc in the same st as the slip st, dc in the next ch-1 sp, *2 dc in the next dc, dc in the next ch-1 sp; repeat from the * around; join with a slip st in the top of the beginning ch-3—36 dc.

Round 4: Ch 4, dc in the next dc, ch 1, skip the next dc, *dc in the next dc, ch 1, dc in the next dc, ch 1, skip the next dc; repeat from the * around; join with a slip st in the third ch of the beginning ch-4—24 dc; 24 ch-1 sps.

Round 5: Ch 3, dc in the same st as the slip st, dc in each of next 3 sts, *2 dc in the next dc, dc in each of next 3 sts ; repeat from the * around; join with a slip st in the top of the beginning ch-3—60 dc.

Round 6: Ch 4, [dc in the next dc, ch 1, skip the next dc] twice, *dc in the next dc, ch 1, [dc in the next dc, ch 1, skip the next dc] twice; repeat from the * around; join with a slip st in the 3rd ch of the beginning ch-4—36 dc; 36 ch-1 sps.

Round 7: Ch 3, dc in the same st as the slip st, dc in each of the next 5 sts, *2 dc in the next dc, dc in

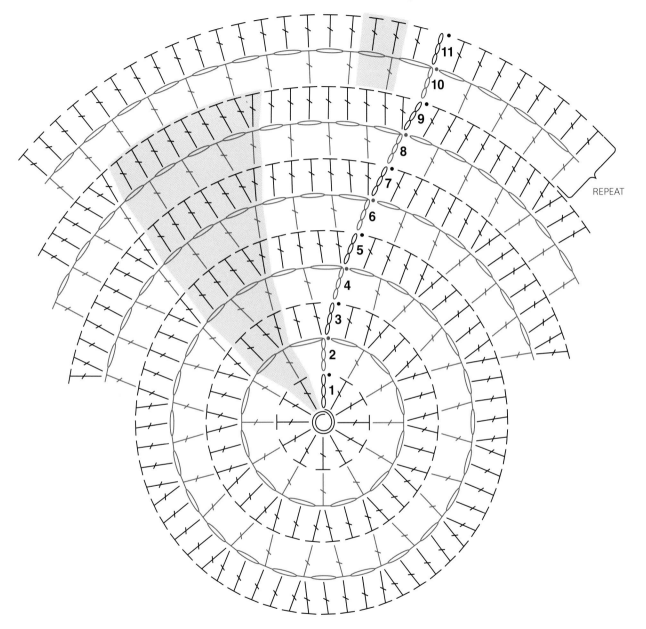

BOTTOM OF BAG THROUGH ROUND 11

REPEAT

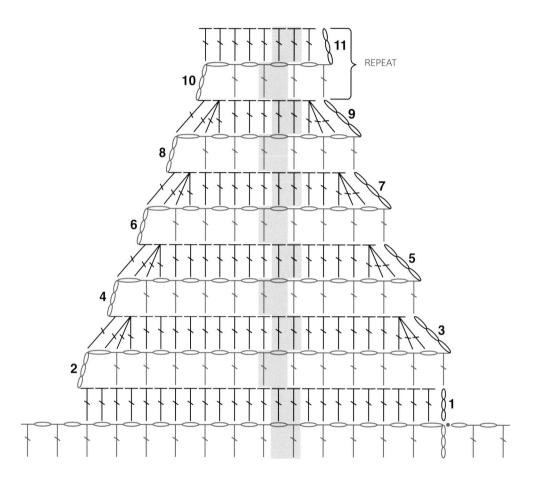

REPEAT

FIRST HANDLE

each of the next 5 sts; repeat from the * around; join with a slip st to the top of the ch-3—84 dc.

Round 8: Ch 4, [dc in the next dc, ch 1, skip the next dc] 3 times, *dc in the next dc, ch 1, [dc in the next dc, ch 1, skip the next dc] 3 times; repeat from the * around; join with a slip st to the third ch of the ch-4—48 dc; 48 ch-1 sps.

Round 9: Ch 3, dc in the same st as the slip st, dc in each of the next 7 sts, *2 dc in the next dc, dc in each of the next 7 sts; repeat from the * around; join with a slip st in the top of the beginning ch-3—108 dc.

Round 10: Ch 4, skip the st where the slip st was worked, skip the next dc, *dc in the next dc, ch 1, skip the next dc; repeat from the * around; join with a slip st to the 3rd ch of the beginning ch-4—48 dc; 48 ch-1 sps.

Round 11: Ch 3, skip the st where the slip st was worked, *dc in the next ch-1 sp, dc in the next dc; repeat from the * around; join with slip st in the 3rd ch of the beginning ch-4—108 dc.

Rounds 12–28: Repeat Rounds 10 and 11 eight times; repeat Round 10 once.

FIRST HANDLE

Work now progresses in rows.

Row 1 (RS): Ch 3, [dc in the next ch-1 sp, dc in the next dc] 12 times, turn, leaving remaining sts unworked—25 dc.

Row 2: Ch 4 (counts as dc, ch 1), skip the first 2 sts, [dc in the next dc, ch 1, skip the next dc] 10 times, dc in the top of the turning-ch-3, turn.

Row 3: Ch 3, skip the first dc, dc3tog over next 3 sts, [dc in the next dc, dc in the next ch-1 sp] 8 times, dc in the next dc, dc3tog over next 3 sts, dc in the third ch of the turning-ch-4, turn.

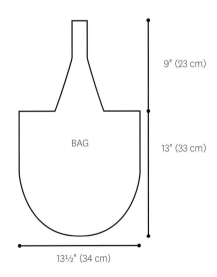

9" (23 cm)

BAG

13" (33 cm)

13½" (34 cm)

Row 4: Ch 4, skip the first 2 sts, [dc in the next dc, ch 1, skip the next dc] 9 times, dc in the top of the turning-ch-3, turn.

Row 5: Ch 3, skip the first dc, dc3tog over next 3 sts, [dc in the next dc, dc in the next ch-1 sp] 6 times, dc in the next dc, dc3tog over next 3 sts, dc in the third ch of the turning-ch-4, turn.

Row 6: Ch 4, skip the first 2 sts of the row, [dc in the next dc, ch 1, skip the next dc] 7 times, dc in the top of the turning-ch-3. Turn.

Row 7: Ch 3, skip the first dc, dc3tog over next 3 sts, [dc in the next dc, dc in the next ch-1 sp] 4 times, dc in the next dc, dc3tog over next 3 sts, dc in the third ch of the turning-ch-4, turn.

Row 8: Ch 4, skip the first 2 sts of the row, [dc in the next dc, ch 1, skip the next dc] 5 times, dc in the top of the turning-ch-3. Turn.

Row 9: Ch 3, skip the first dc, dc3tog over next 3 sts, [dc in the next dc, dc in the next ch-1 sp] twice, dc in the next dc, dc3tog over next 3 sts, dc in the third ch of the turning-ch-4, turn.

Row 10: Ch 4, skip the first 2 sts of the row, [dc in the next dc, ch 1, skip the next dc] 3 times, dc in the top of the turning-ch-3, turn.

Row 11: Ch 3, [dc in the next ch-1 sp, dc in the next dc] 3 times, dc under the turning-ch-4, dc in the third ch of the turning-ch-4, turn.

Rows 12–17: Repeat Rows 10 and 11 three times. Fasten off, leaving a sewing length.

SECOND HANDLE

With the RS facing, skip 29 sts from the left-hand edge of the First Handle, join yarn with a slip st to the next dc.

Row 1 (RS): Ch 3, [dc in the next ch-1 sp, dc in the next dc] 12 times, turn, leaving remaining sts unworked—25 dc.

Complete same as the First Handle.

FINISHING

Matching sts, sew the last rows of handles together.

Weave in ends.

ORO

COWL/PONCHINI

Made in the round with airy V-stitches, this versatile

accessory can be worn as either a cowl or a ponchini.

+
SIZE

Small/Medium
(Large/1X, 2X/3X).
Instructions are for
the smallest size,
with changes for
larger sizes noted
in parentheses,
as necessary.

+
FINISHED
MEASUREMENTS

13" (33 cm) deep ×
34 (39, 44½)"
(86.5 [99, 113] cm)
in circumference

+
MATERIALS

• Berroco *Flicker*
(4)
(87% baby alpaca/
8% acrylic/5% other
fibers; each approximately
1.75 oz/50 g and 189
yd/175 m), 3 hanks of
Svetlana #3340

• Crochet hook size
J/10 (6 mm) or size
needed to obtain
the gauge

+
GAUGE

4 V-sts and 6 rows in the
pattern = 2½" (6.25 cm),
blocked. To save time,
take time to check gauge.

+
ALTERNATIVE
YARN CHOICE

Cascade *Eco Alpaca*

$\bigvee$ O T E
• V-Stitch (V-st) = [Dc, ch 1, dc] in the indicated st or sp

COWL/PONCHINI

Loosely chain 166 (190, 214).

Join with a slip st to form a ring, being careful not to twist.

Foundation Round (RS): V-st in the fifth ch from the hook, *skip the next 2 ch, V-st in the next ch; repeat from the * around, ending with slip st to the top of beginning ch-3—55 (63, 71) V-sts.

Round 1: Ch 3, V-st in each V-st around; join with a slip st in the top of the beginning ch-3.

Repeat Round 1 until the piece measures approximately 13" (33 cm) from the beginning. Fasten off.

FINISHING

Weave in ends. Block to the finished measurements.

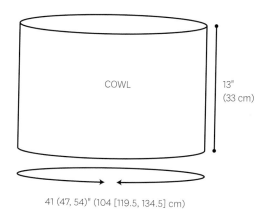

COWL   13" (33 cm)

41 (47, 54)" (104 [119.5, 134.5] cm)

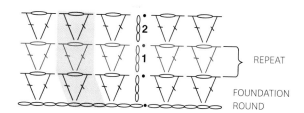

REPEAT

FOUNDATION ROUND

MONTERRA

BOOT TOPPERS

Keep warm in style with these adorable boot toppers. Since they are stitched in a simple shell pattern with bulky yarn, you'll have them whipped up in no time!

+

SIZES

Small/Medium (Medium/Large). Instructions are for the smaller size, with changes for the larger size noted in parentheses, as necessary.

+

FINISHED MEASUREMENTS

13" (33 cm) deep × 16 (18)" (40.5 [45.5] cm) in circumference at bottom edge; 18 (20)" (45.5 [51] cm) in circumference at top edge

+

MATERIALS

• Brown Sheep Company *Lamb's Pride Bulky* Ⓢ (85% wool/15% mohair; each approximately 4 oz/113 g and 125 yd/114 m), 3 skeins of #M10 Creme

• Crochet hooks sizes J/10 (6 mm) and K/10.5 (6.5 mm) or sizes needed to obtain the gauge

+

GAUGE

With the smaller hook, 1 repeat (shell, FPdc) = 2¼" (5.5 cm); 3 rows = 2½" (6.25 cm). With the larger hook, 1 repeat (shell, FPdc) = 2½" (6.25 cm). To save time, take time to check gauge.

+

ALTERNATIVE YARN CHOICE

Lion Brand *Alpine Wool*

SPECIAL STITCHES

Shell = [3 dc, ch 1, 3 dc] in same st or sp.

Picot = Ch 3, slip st in 3rd ch from hook.

BOOT TOPPER

With the smaller hook, ch 42 (48). Join with a slip st to form a ring, being careful not to twist.

Foundation Round (WS): Ch 3 (counts as dc here and throughout), shell in 6th ch from the hook, *skip the next 2 ch, dc in the next ch, skip the next 2 ch, shell in the next ch; repeat from the * around, ending with skip the next 2 ch, slip st to the top of the beginning ch-3—7 (8) shells.

Round 1 (WS): Ch 2, skip the first 3 dc, *shell in the

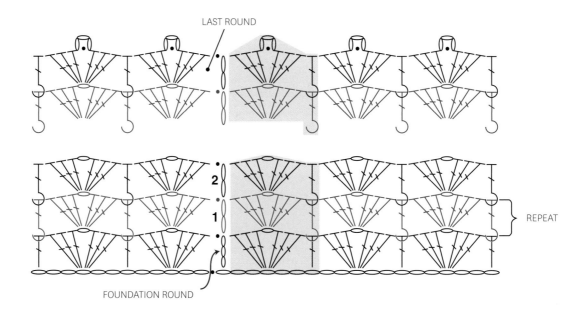

LAST ROUND

2

1

REPEAT

FOUNDATION ROUND

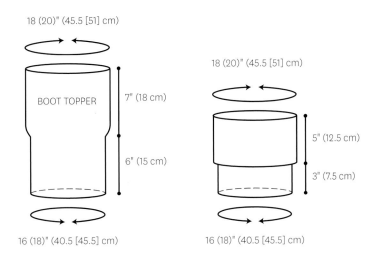

18 (20)" (45.5 [51] cm)

BOOT TOPPER

7" (18 cm)

6" (15 cm)

16 (18)" (40.5 [45.5] cm)

18 (20)" (45.5 [51] cm)

5" (12.5 cm)

3" (7.5 cm)

16 (18)" (40.5 [45.5] cm)

next ch-1 sp, skip the next 3 dc, FPdc in the next st; repeat from the *around, ending with shell in the last ch-1 sp; join with a slip st in the top of the beginning ch-2.

Repeat Round 1 until the piece measures approximately 6" (15 cm) from the beginning.

Change to the larger hook, and repeat Round 1 until the piece measures approximately 13" (33 cm) from the beginning.

Last Round: Ch 2, skip the first 3 dc, *[3 dc, picot, 3 dc] in the next ch-1 sp, skip the next 3 dc, FPdc in the next st; repeat from the *around, ending with [3 dc, picot, 3 dc] in the next ch-1 sp; join with a slip st in the top of the beginning ch-2. Fasten off.

FINISHING

Weave in ends. Block to the finished measurements.

Fold the upper section 5" (12.5 cm) to the RS so that post sts are raised to RS.

ASHLEY

HEADBAND

Keep your ears warm with this headband. The Greek key pattern is made using just one color per row. Try it! It is a lot easier than it looks!

+
SIZE
One size

+
FINISHED MEASUREMENTS
4" (10 cm) wide ×
20" (51 cm) in
circumference
Width: 4" (10 cm)

+
MATERIALS
• Premier Yarns
Downton Abbey Matthew
(75% acrylic/21% wool/
4% viscose; each
approximately
3.5 oz/100 g and
230 yd/210 m),
1 skein each of #01
Dusky Mauve (A)
and #03 Birch White (B)

• Crochet hook size
I/9 (5.5 mm) or size
needed to obtain gauge

+
GAUGE
12 sts and 16 rows
in pattern = 4" (10 cm).
To save time, take time
to check gauge.

+
**ALTERNATIVE
YARN CHOICE**
Paton's *Decor*

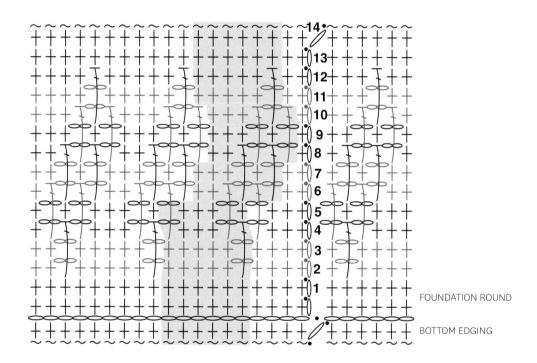

FOUNDATION ROUND

BOTTOM EDGING

$$N O T E S$$

- This project is worked in the round with the right side facing at all times.

- For ease in finishing, do not cut the yarn at the end of each two-row stripe; instead, carry the yarns loosely up the wrong side until needed again.

HEADBAND

With A, chain 57. Join with a slip st to form a ring, being careful not to twist.

Foundation Round (RS): Ch 1, sc in each ch around; join with a slip st in the first sc—60 sc.

Round 1 (RS): Ch 1, sc in each sc around; join with a slip st in the first sc. Change to B.

Round 2: Ch 1, sc in each of the first 4 sc, *ch 2, skip the next sc, sc in each of the next 5 sc; repeat from the * around, ending with ch 2, skip the next sc, sc in last sc; join with a slip st in the first sc.

Round 3: Ch 1, sc in each of the first 4 sc, *ch 2, skip the next ch-2 sp, sc in each of the next 5 sc; repeat from the * around, ending with ch 2, skip next sc, sc in the last sc; join with a slip st in the first sc. Change to A.

Round 4: With A, ch 1, sc in each of the first 3 sc, ch 2, skip the next sc, *dc in the next skipped sc 3 rows below, ch 2, skip the next sc**, sc in each of the next 3 sc, ch 2, skip the next sc; repeat from the * around, ending the last repeat at **; join with a slip st in the first sc.

Round 5: Ch 1, sc in each of the first 3 sc, ch 2, skip the next ch-2 sp, *sc in the next dc, ch 2, skip the next ch-2 sp**, sc in each of the next 3 sc, ch 2, skip the next ch-2 sp; repeat from the * around, ending the last repeat at **; join with a slip st in the first sc. Change to B.

Round 6: With B, ch 1, sc in each of the first 2 sc, *ch 2, skip the next sc, dc in the next skipped sc 3 rows below, ch 2, skip the next sc, dc in the next skipped sc 3 rows below**, sc in each of the next 2 sc; repeat from the * around, ending the last repeat at **; join with a slip st in the first sc.

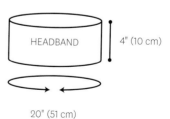

HEADBAND   4" (10 cm)

20" (51 cm)

Round 7: Ch 1, sc in each of the first 2 sts, *ch 2, skip the next ch-2 sp, sc in next dc, ch 2, skip the next ch-2 sp**, sc in each of the next 3 sts; repeat from the * around, ending the last repeat at **, sc in last dc; join with a slip st in the first sc. Change to A.

Round 8: With A, ch 1, sc in the first sc, *[ch 2, skip the next sc, dc in the next skipped sc 3 rows below] twice**, sc in each of the next 2 sc; repeat from the * around, ending the last repeat at **, sc in the last sc; join with a slip st in the first sc.

Round 9: Ch 1, sc in the first sc, *ch 2, skip the next ch-2 sp, sc in next dc, ch 2, skip the next ch-2 sp**, sc in each of the next 3 sts; repeat from the * around, ending the last repeat at **, sc in each of last 2 sts; join with a slip st in the first sc. Change to B.

Round 10: With B, ch 1, sc in the first sc, *dc in the next skipped sc 3 rows below, ch 2, skip the next sc, dc in the next skipped sc 3 rows below**, sc in each of the next 3 sc; repeat from the * around, ending the last repeat at **, sc in each of last 2 sc; join with a slip st in the first sc.

Round 11: Ch 1, sc in each of the first sc, *ch 2, skip the next ch-2 sp**, sc in each of the next 5 sts; repeat from the * around, ending the last repeat at **, sc in each of last 3 sts; join with a slip st in the first sc. Change to A. Ch 1.

Round 12: With A, ch 1, sc in each of the first 2 sc, *dc in the next skipped sc 3 rows below, sc in each of the next 5 sc; repeat from the * around, ending the last repeat at **, sc in each of the last 3 sts; join with a slip st in the first sc.

Round 13: Ch 1, sc in each st around; join with a slip st in the first sc.

Round 14: Ch 1, *working from left to right*, reverse sc (page 135) in each st around; join with a slip st in first reverse sc. Fasten off.

Bottom Edging (RS): With RS facing, *working across opposite side of the Foundation Ch*, join A with a slip st in any ch, ch 1, working from left to right, reverse sc in each st around; join with a slip st in first reverse sc. Fasten off.

FINISHING

Weave in ends.

ELISSE

BUTTON NECKLACE

Once you make this necklace for yourself, all your friends are going to want one! It is made with super simple chain stitches and novelty buttons.

+

SIZE

One size

+

FINISHED MEASUREMENTS

20" (51 cm) long, but can easily be made in different lengths by adding more buttons

+

MATERIALS

For the brown necklace:
• Universal Yarn *Garden 10* (100% Egyptian mercerized cotton; each approximately 1.75 oz/50 g and 306 yd/ 280 m), 1 ball of #700-28 Chocolate

• Steel crochet hook size 7 (1.5 mm) or size needed to obtain gauge

• 11 Assorted two-hole buttons (One World Button Supply NPL 200-26HB, GHB 131-A, GHB 131-PK, and NPL 269-15HB were used in sample project)

For the star necklace:
• Coats & Clark *South Maid Crochet Thread*, Size 10 (100% mercerized cotton; each approximately 400 yd/125 m), 1 ball of #429 Ecru

• One size 7 (1.5 mm) steel crochet hook or size needed to obtain gauge

• 11 assorted two-hole buttons (One World Button Supply SPN 116-24 White, NPL 208-22H, NPL 374-20B, and NPL 374-20P were used in sample project)

+

GAUGE

Approximately 8 ch sts = ½" (1.3 cm). Gauge is not crucial to the success of this project.

+

ALTERNATIVE YARN CHOICE

Omega/Tamm *Cotton Thread*, Size 10

$\mathsf{N\,O\,T\,E}$ • When working the slip sts into the buttons, keep the thread beneath the button (page 137).

NECKLACE

Arrange buttons in a pleasing order. Make a slip knot, and insert the hook in the loop.

*Slip st in the first hole of one button, slip st in the second hole of the same button, ch 7; repeat from the * until 10 buttons have been attached, ending with slip st in the first st of last button, slip st in the 2nd hole of the same button. *Do not fasten off.*

CLOSURE

Ch 18, slip st in the eleventh ch from the hook. Fasten off.

FINISHING

Weave in ends.

CLOSURE

START

REDUCED SAMPLE OF PATTERN

RESOURCES

IN THIS SECTION, YOU'LL FIND INFORMATION ABOUT CROCHET INSTRUCTIONS AND CHARTS, VARIOUS TECHNIQUES, AND THE CROCHET COMMUNITY—EVERYTHING YOU NEED TO KNOW TO ENJOY USING THIS BOOK.

ABBREVIATIONS LIST

NOTE
- American terms are used throughout this book. For UK equivalents, refer to the chart to the right.

AMERICAN TERM	UK TERM
double crochet (dc)	treble crochet (tr)
double triple crochet (dtr)	triple treble crochet (tr tr)
gauge	tension
half double crochet (hdc)	half treble crochet (htr)
single crochet (sc)	double crochet (dc)
slip stitch	single crochet (sc)
triple crochet (tr)	double treble crochet (dtr)
yarn over	yarn over hook (YOH)

BPdc — back post double crochet stitch

BPtr — back post triple crochet stitch

ch(s) — chain(s)

ch sp — chain space

dc — double crochet stitch

dec — decrease

dtr — double triple crochet stitch

FPdc — front post double crochet stitch

FPdtr — front post double triple crochet stitch

FPst(s) — front post stitch(es)

FPtr — front post triple crochet stitch

hdc — half double crochet stitch

PB — Place bead (slide bead close to the last stitch made)

RS — right side

sc — single crochet stitch

sp(s) — space(s)

st(s) — stitch(es)

tr — triple crochet stitch

WS — wrong side

* — repeat the instructions after the asterisk or between the asterisks across the row or for as many times as instructed

[ ] — repeat the instructions within the parentheses for as many times as instructed

UNDERSTANDING INTERNATIONAL CROCHET SYMBOLS

The charts in this book use the standard symbols commonly understood by crocheters all over the world. Here's how to use them to make your stitching easier, quicker, and more fun!

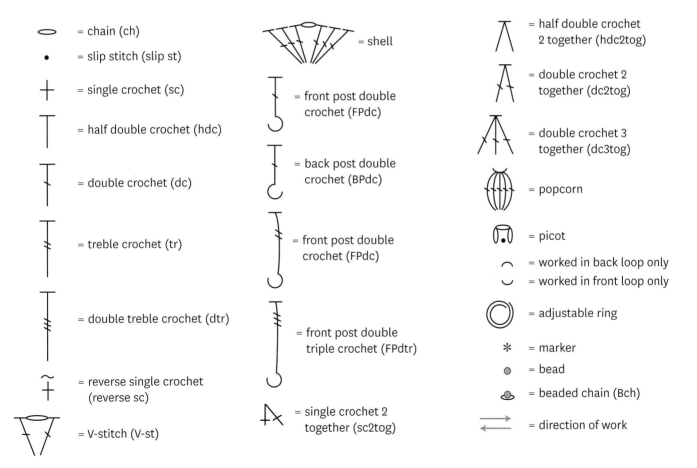

= chain (ch)

= slip stitch (slip st)

= single crochet (sc)

= half double crochet (hdc)

= double crochet (dc)

= treble crochet (tr)

= double treble crochet (dtr)

= reverse single crochet (reverse sc)

= V-stitch (V-st)

= shell

= front post double crochet (FPdc)

= back post double crochet (BPdc)

= front post double crochet (FPdc)

= front post double triple crochet (FPdtr)

= single crochet 2 together (sc2tog)

= half double crochet 2 together (hdc2tog)

= double crochet 2 together (dc2tog)

= double crochet 3 together (dc3tog)

= popcorn

= picot

= worked in back loop only
= worked in front loop only

= adjustable ring

= marker

= bead

= beaded chain (Bch)

= direction of work

TIPS ON READING THE CROCHET CHARTS

The Foundation Chain is shown at the bottom of each picture, and each successive row is added from the bottom up, in the order they are crocheted. Rows are clearly numbered to help you keep track of your place in the pattern.

Right-side rows are shown in black and are read from right to left; wrong-side rows are shown in blue and are read from left to right.

The stitch repeat (or multiple) is highlighted in gray.

The row repeat is indicated with brackets.

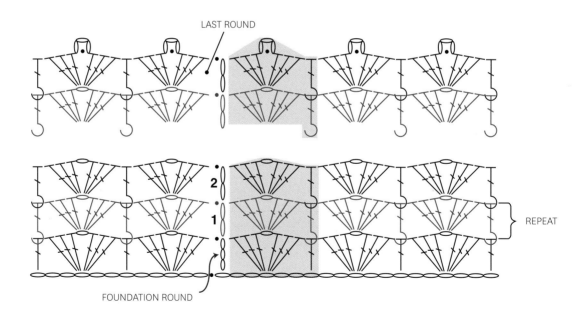

LAST ROUND

2

1

REPEAT

FOUNDATION ROUND

GENERAL CROCHET TECHNIQUES

BASIC STITCHES

SLIP KNOT

Beginning at least 6" (15 cm) from the end of the yarn, make a loose loop, laying the loop on top of the yarn as it comes out of the ball. Use the crochet hook to grab the yarn, and tighten the loop to fit snuggly on the hook.

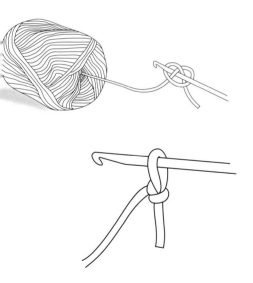

ADJUSTABLE RING

Wrap yarn clockwise around left index finger, insert hook under loop around finger, yarnover hook, draw yarn through loop on finger, yarn over, draw yarn through loop on hook for first chain.

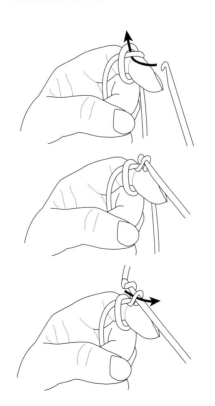

CHAIN (abbreviated ch)

Place a slip knot on your hook. Yarn over the hook and draw it through the loop on the hook to form the first chain. Repeat this step as many times as required.

NOTE
- In patterns, the loop on the hook is not included when counting the number of chain stitches.

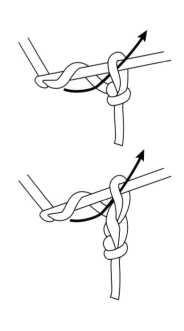

TURNING-CHAINS

At the end of each row or round, a turning-chain is used to bring the hook and yarn to the height required for working the next row or round. A row of single crochet stitches, for example, has the same height as a single chain stitch, so before moving from one row of single crochet to another, you must chain one stitch to turn.

In all cases except single crochet, the turning-chain counts as the first stitch of the next row. After chaining three stitches to turn for a row of double crochet, for instance, you would insert your hook in the second stitch of the row; your last double crochet stitch would be worked in the top of the turning-chain-3 at the end of the row.

Refer to the chart below for recommended turning-chain heights.

CROCHET STITCH	CORRESPONDING TURNING-CHAIN
Single crochet	Chain one
Half-double crochet	Chain two
Double crochet	Chain three
Triple crochet	Chain four
Double triple crochet	Chain five

SLIP STITCH
(abbreviated slip st)

Insert the hook in the indicated stitch, yarn over the hook and draw it through both the stitch and the loop on the hook.

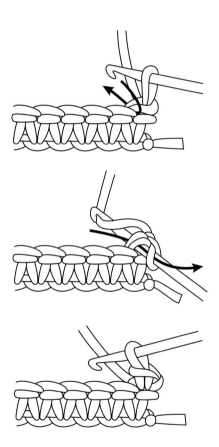

SINGLE CROCHET
(abbreviated sc)

Insert the hook in the indicated stitch, yarn over the hook and pull up a loop (2 loops are on your hook); yarn over the hook and draw it through both loops on the hook.

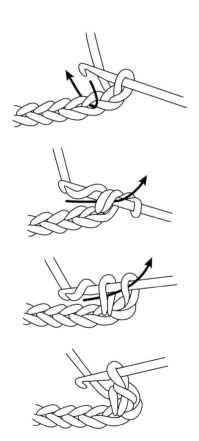

HALF DOUBLE CROCHET
(abbreviated hdc)

Yarn over the hook, insert the hook in the indicated stitch, yarn over the hook and pull up a loop (3 loops are on your hook); yarn over the hook and draw it through all 3 loops on the hook.

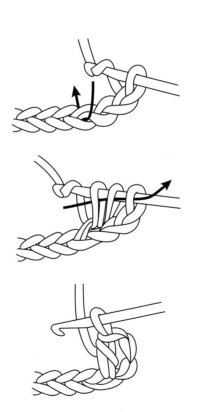

DOUBLE CROCHET
(abbreviated dc)

Yarn over the hook, insert the hook in the indicated stitch, yarn over the hook and pull up a loop (3 loops are on your hook); [yarn over the hook and draw it through 2 loops on the hook] twice.

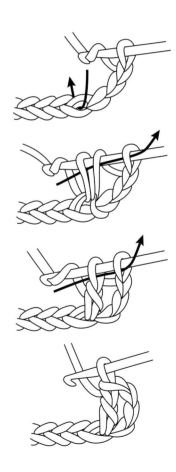

TRIPLE CROCHET
(abbreviated tr)

[Yarn over the hook] twice, insert the hook in the indicated stitch, yarn over the hook and pull up a loop (4 loops are on your hook); [yarn over hook and draw it through 2 loops on the hook] 3 times.

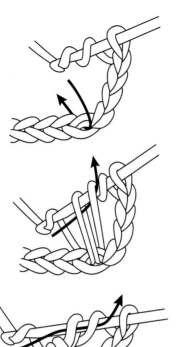

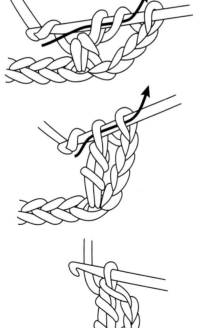

DOUBLE TRIPLE CROCHET
(abbreviated dtr)

[Yarn over the hook] 3 times, insert the hook in the indicated stitch and pull up a loop (5 loops are on your hook); [yarn over the hook and draw it through 2 loops on the hook] 4 times.

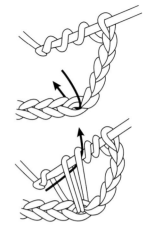

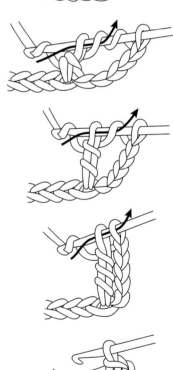

STITCH VARIATIONS

BEADED CHAIN (Bch)

Slide a bead up close to the last st made, yarn over, draw yarn through loop.

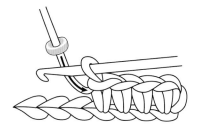

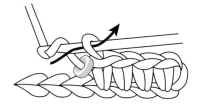

SINGLE CROCHET 2 TOGETHER
(abbreviated sc2tog)

[Insert the hook in the next stitch, yarn over, draw up a loop] twice, yarn over and draw loop through all 3 loops on hook.

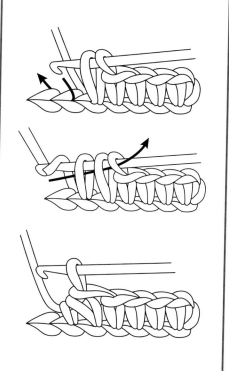

HALF DOUBLE CROCHET 2 TOGETHER (hdc2tog)

[Yarn over, insert the hook in the next st, yarn over, draw up a loop] twice, yarn over, draw through 5 loops on hook.

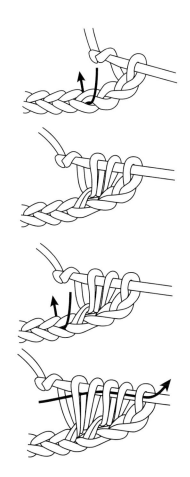

DOUBLE CROCHET 2 TOGETHER (dc2tog)

Yarn over, insert the hook in the next st and pull up a loop; yarn over and draw yarn through 2 loops on hook, yarn over; insert the hook in the next st and pull up a loop, yarn over and draw yarn through 2 loops on hook, yarn over, draw through 3 loops on hook.

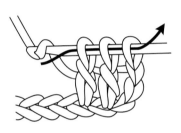

DOUBLE CROCHET 3 TOGETHER (dc3tog)

Yarn over, insert the hook in next st and pull up a loop (3 loops are on your hook); yarn over and draw through 2 loops on the hook; [yarn over, insert hook in next st and pull up a loop; yarn over and draw it through 2 loops on the hook] twice, yarn over the hook and draw loop through all 4 loops on hook.

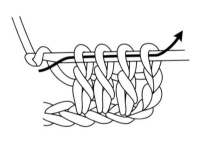

5-DC POPCORN

Work 5 double crochet stitches in a stitch or space; drop the loop from the hook; reinsert the hook in the first double crochet stitch made, pick up the dropped loop and pull it through the first double crochet stitch.

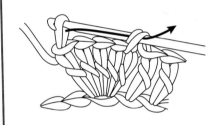

REVERSE SINGLE CROCHET
(reverse sc)

Working from left to right, insert hook in next stitch, yarn over, draw up a loop; yarn over and draw loop through both loops on hook.

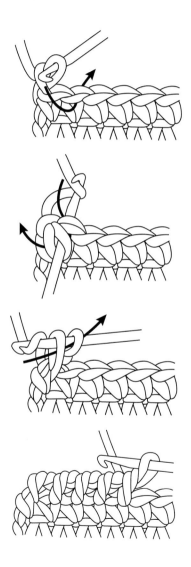

WORKING AROUND THE FRONT POST OF A STITCH

(as for Front Post Double Crochet (FPdc) or Front Post Triple Crochet (FPtr) stitches) Instead of working stitch in the top of the row below, *insert the hook from front to back to front* around the post of the indicated stitch in the row below, as shown in the illustration below, and complete the stitch the ordinary way.

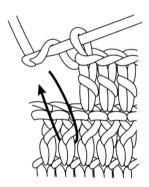

WORKING AROUND THE BACK POST OF A STITCH

(as in Back Post Double Crochet (BPdc) or Back Post Triple Crochet (BPtr) stitches) Instead of working stitch in the top of the row below, insert the hook *from back to front to back* around the post of the indicated stitch in the row below, as shown in the illustration below, and complete the stitch the ordinary way.

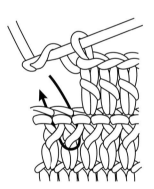

WORKING BEHIND THE LAST ROW

Keeping the last row to the front, work a stitch in the indicated stitch one or more rows below.

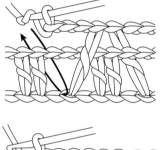

WORKING IN FRONT OF A CHAIN SPACE OF THE PREVIOUS ROW

Keeping the chain space of the previous row to the back of the fabric, work a stitch in the indicated stitch one or more rows below.

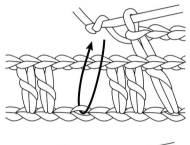

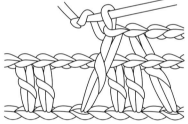

WORKING IN THE BACK OR FRONT LOOP ONLY

Rather than working in both loops of the indicated stitch, insert the hook *under the back or front loop only*, and complete the stitch the ordinary way.

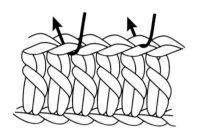

WORKING OVER A CHAIN SPACE

Make a stitch in the stitch or space the indicated number of rows below, enclosing the chain space inside the new stitch.

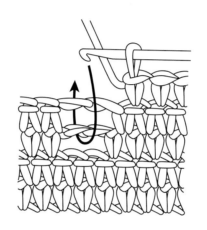

SLIP ST INTO BUTTON

Insert hook in first hole of button, yarn over, draw yarn through the hole, then draw yarn through the loop on hook.

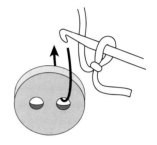

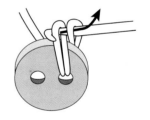

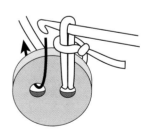

WORKING WITH COLOR

ATTACHING A NEW COLOR OR NEW BALL OF YARN

Work the last stitch of the old color or ball of yarn until two loops are on the hook, then, leaving a 6" (15 cm) tail, use the new color or ball of yarn to complete the stitch.

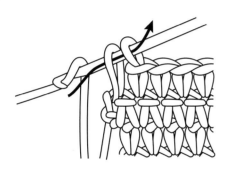

CARRYING THE YARN ALONG THE SIDE OF THE FABRIC

To minimize the number of yarn tails left to be darned in, yarns can be *loosely* carried up the edge of the fabric when working an even number of rows per stripe.

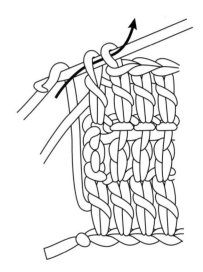

FINISHING TECHNIQUES

WHIPSTITCH SEAM

Use this technique for an especially strong seam.

Lay the pieces flat with the right sides facing you. Use a blunt-tip yarn needle to sew them together as shown in the illustration.

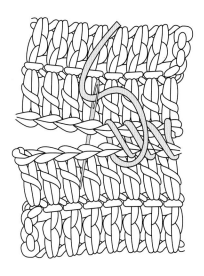

MATTRESS STITCH SEAM

Use this technique when an invisible seam is desired. It's like magic!

With RS facing you, pin the two pieces together, carefully matching patterns and stripes, if necessary. Thread a blunt tip yarn needle with your sewing yarn. Bring the needle up from back to front through the lower right-hand corner of the left-hand piece of fabric, leaving a 6" (15 cm) tail. Bring the yarn up and through the bottom edge of the first stitch on the right-hand piece to secure the lower edges. Bring the yarn up and through the first stitch on the left-hand piece *from front to back to front*. Be sure to go under strands in the center of stitches to create a sturdy seam. Insert the needle in the corresponding place on the right-hand piece *from front to back to front*.

Repeat the last 2 steps, catching the side stitches of each piece until the seam is completed. After you have joined several rows, pull tautly on the seaming yarn, allowing one half of each edge stitch to roll to the wrong side to form a seam.

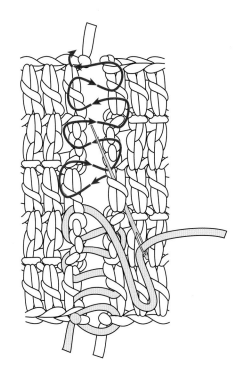

BLOCKING

Prior to seaming your crocheted pieces, take the time to block them in shape. This simple process can dramatically improve the appearance of your projects and can tame even the most unruly stitches! To do it, use the instruction on the yarn label to launder your project pieces, then use rustless pins to shape the damp fabric to the desired measurements and allow it to dry flat. Or gently steam the pieces in shape by placing a damp cloth over them and then carefully wafting a hot steam iron just above the fabric. Don't actually touch the iron to the fabric or you'll risk flattening it. (Don't ask me how I know!)

FASTEN OFF

Cut yarn leaving a 6" (15 cm) tail, yarn over, draw yarn all the way through loop on hook, pull tail to tighten.

WEAVE IN ENDS

One by one, thread yarn ends through a pointed-end yarn needle and make short running stitches on the wrong side of your fabric in a diagonal line for about one inch or so, piercing the yarn strands that comprise the stitches of your fabric (illustrations 1 and 2). Then, stitch back to where you began, working alongside your previous running stitches (illustration 3). Finally, to secure the tail, work a stitch or two and actually pierce the running stitches you just created. Be sure to work each tail individually, in opposite diagonal directions, and you will secure your yarn ends while keeping the public side of your fabric neat and beautiful.

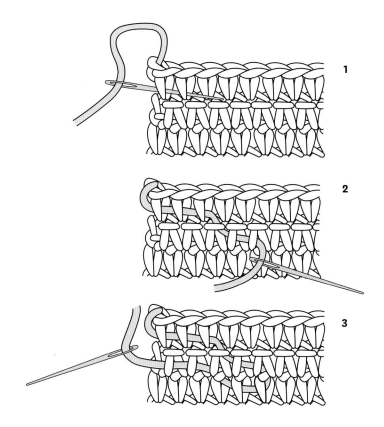

MATERIAL RESOURCES

I always recommend purchasing supplies at your local yarn shop. If there isn't one in your area, contact the appropriate wholesaler below for more information.

Berroco Yarn
1 Tupperware Drive, Suite 4,
N. Smithfield, RI 02896-6815
(401) 769-1212
www.berroco.com

Brown Sheep Company
100662 County Road 16
Mitchell, NE 69357
1-800-826-9136
www.brownsheep.com

Cascade Yarns
1224 Andover Park E
Tukwila, WA 98188
(206) 574-0440
www.cascadeyarns.com

Classic Elite Yarns
16 Esquire Road, Unit 2
North Billerica, MA 01862-2500
1-800-343-0308
www.classiceliteyarns.com

Coats & Clark
Consumer Services
P.O. Box 12229
Greenville, SC 29612-0229
(800) 648-1479
www.makeitcoats.com

Koigu Wool Designs
Box 158
Chatsworth, ON, N0H 1G0
Canada
(519) 794-3066
www.koigu.com

Lion Brand Yarn
135 Kero Road
Carlstadt, NJ 07072
(800) 258-9276
www.lionbrand.com

Patons Yarn
320 Livingstone Avenue South
Box 40
Listowel, ON, N4W 3H3
Canada
(888) 368-8401
www.yarnspirations.com

Plymouth Yarn Company, Inc
500 Lafayette Street
Bristol, PA 19007
(215) 788-0459
www.plymouthyarn.com

Red Heart (see Coats & Clark)

South Maid (see Coats & Clark)

Universal Yarn
5991 Caldwell Business Park Drive
Harrisburg, NC 28075
(704) 789-9276
www.universalyarn.com

YARN WEIGHTS AND SUBSTITUTIONS

Each project in this book was designed for a specific yarn. Different yarns possess their own characteristics, which will affect the way they appear and behave when crocheted. To duplicate the projects exactly as photographed, I suggest that you use the designated yarns. Even so, you'll find that the nature of any handmade project assures subtle differences and variances.

However, if you would like to make a yarn substitution, be sure to choose a yarn whose weight is similar to the one called for in the pattern. Yarn sizes and weights are usually indicated on the label, but for an accurate test, crochet a swatch using the recommended hook size, making it at least 4" (10 cm) square. Count the number of stitches in the swatch and refer to the table below to determine the yarn's weight.

CRAFT YARN COUNCIL OF AMERICA	0 LACE	1 SUPER FINE	2 FINE	3 LIGHT	4 MEDIUM	5 BULKY	6 SUPER BULKY	7 JUMBO
YARN WEIGHTS	Fingering, 10-count crochet thread	Sock, Fingering, Baby	Sport, Baby	DK, Light Worsted	Worsted, Afghan, Aran	Chunky, Craft, Rug	Super Bulky, Roving	Jumbo, Roving
AVERAGE GAUGE IN SINGLE CROCHET TO 4" (10 CM)[1]	32 to 42 double crochets[2]	21 to 32 sts	16 to 20 sts	12 to 17 sts	11 to 14 sts	8 to 11 sts	7 to 9 sts	6 sts and fewer
RECOMMENDED HOOK U.S. SIZE RANGE	Steel[3] 6, 7, 8; regular hook B-1	B-1 to E-4	E-4 to 7	7 to I-9	I-9 to K-10-1/2	K-10-1/2 to M-13	M-13 to Q	Q and larger
RECOMMENDED HOOK METRIC SIZE RANGE	Steel[3] 1.6 to 1.4 mm; regular hook 2.25 mm	2.25 to 3.5 mm	3.5 to 4.5 mm	4.5 to 5.5 mm	5.5 to 6.5 mm	6.5 to 9 mm	9 to 15 mm	15 mm and larger

1. The above reflect the most commonly used gauges and hook sizes for specific yarn categories.

2. Lace-weight yarns are usually crocheted on larger hooks to create lacy, openwork pattern. Accordingly, a gauge range is difficult to determine. Always follow the gauge stated in the pattern.

3. Steel crochet hooks are sized differently from regular hooks—the higher the number, the smaller the hook, which is the reverse of regular hook sizing.

THE CROCHET COMMUNITY

To meet other crocheters and to learn more about the craft, contact this wonderful nonprofit organization:

The Crochet Guild of America
1100-H Brandywine Boulevard
Zanesville, OH 43701-7303
(740) 452-4541
www.crochet.org

To meet other crocheters online, visit

www.ravelry.com

Join my fan group on Ravelry to share photos of your projects and to keep up with my work. Go to http://www.ravelry.com/groups/melissa-leapman-rocks to be part of the fun!

Join my online classes on Craftsy.com! Use this link to get 50% off any of my classes:
http://craftsy.me/29sAXRr

ABOUT THE AUTHOR

With more than 1,000 designs in print, **Melissa Leapman** is one of the most widely published knitwear and crochet designers. Working with leading ready-to-wear design houses and top yarn companies and the author of many authoritative books on knitting and crochet, Leapman is also a well-respected teacher who teaches classes and workshops at yarn and fiber shows, at knitting and crochet guild events, and at yarn shops both nationally and internationally. She lives in New York City.